NBA POWER Conditioning

National Basketball Conditioning Coaches Association

Human Kinetics

Library of Congress Cataloging-in-Publication Data

National Basketball Conditioning Coaches Association.
    NBA power conditioning / National Basketball Conditioning Coaches
Association.
        p.   cm.
    Includes bibliographical references (p. 202).
    ISBN 0-88011-687-0
    1. Basketball--Training.   2. Physical fitness.   I. Title.
GV885.35.N38   1997
613.7' 11--dc21   97-19426
                                                                     CIP

ISBN: 0-88011-687-0

Developmental Editor: Chad A. Johnson; **Managing Editor:** Alesha G. Thompson; **Editorial Assistants:** Laura Majersky and Amy Carnes; **Copyeditor:** Bob Replinger; **Proofreader:** Pam Johnson; **Graphic Designer:** Bob Reuther; **Graphic Artist:** Francine Hamerski; **Photo Editor:** Boyd LaFoon; **Cover Designer:** Jack Davis; **Photographer (cover):** NBA Photos/Victor Baldizon; **Illustrators:** Tim Ladwig, M.R. Greenberg, and Keith Blomberg; **Printer:** Versa Press

Human Kinetics books are available at special discounts for bulk purchase. Special editions or book excerpts can also be created to specification. For details, contact the Special Sales Manager at Human Kinetics.

Printed in the United States of America   10 9 8 7 6 5 4 3 2

Human Kinetics
Web site: http://www.humankinetics.com/

United States: Human Kinetics, P.O. Box 5076, Champaign, IL 61825-5076
1-800-747-4457
e-mail: humank@hkusa.com

Canada: Human Kinetics, Box 24040, Windsor, ON N8Y 4Y9
1-800-465-7301 (in Canada only)
e-mail: humank@hkcanada.com

Europe: Human Kinetics, P.O. Box IW14, Leeds LS16 6TR, United Kingdom
(44) 1132 781708
e-mail: humank@hkeurope.com

Australia: Human Kinetics, 57A Price Avenue, Lower Mitcham, South Australia 5062
(08) 277 1555
e-mail: humank@hkaustralia.com

New Zealand: Human Kinetics, P.O. Box 105-231, Auckland 1
(09) 523 3462
e-mail: humank@hknewz.com

We would like to thank the many NBA players who permitted us to photograph them for this book and who were so generous in providing their insights on conditioning and its importance to their careers.

CONTENTS

FOREWORD

If you want to perform at the peak of your abilities, then you must prepare yourself mentally, emotionally, and most of all, physically.

An athlete who takes the time to condition his or her body is more ready to meet the challenges of competition and, therefore, succeed at a higher rate. Everyone is aware that strength and conditioning programs have become very sophisticated today. Wise athletes will take advantage of the detailed programs described in this book.

Lenny Wilkens
Atlanta Hawks head coach
NBA Coach of the Year, 1994
USA men's Olympic team head coach, 1996
All-time winningest NBA head coach

INTRODUCTION
ADDING POWER TO YOUR GAME

Now, more than ever, we know what it takes to be a superbly conditioned basketball player. At the pro and major-college levels you can see how that knowledge has changed the physical makeup and moves of athletes. Compare the often skinny and sometimes slow players of the '60s and '70s to the high-powered players of the '90s, and you'll see how much bigger, stronger, and faster athletes are now.

The problem is that the physical-conditioning information and programs that produced today's elite basketball athletes have been effectively shared with only a small portion of players and coaches at the college, high school, and middle school levels. We, the National Basketball Conditioning Coaches Association, wanted to change that.

In *NBA Power Conditioning*, NBA conditioning coaches make all aspects of training clear and understandable. Even more important to you, we present exercises, drills, workouts, programs, and a nutritional plan that you can use to become a highly conditioned, more powerful, and better basketball player.

The book is divided into three parts. Part I is titled "Power Preparation." The first chapter emphasizes how to improve flexibility and take care of your body before and after workouts to improve performance and help prevent injury. In chapter 2 we provide nutritional guidance to help improve conditioning and performance. At that point, you're ready for chapter 3, which outlines the year-round conditioning guidelines, including an off-season program to establish the conditioning base for preseason practice.

Part II, "Power Base Strength," shows how to put more muscle on your bones and in your game. If you're unable to shoot the three-pointer with ease or outmuscle opponents for rebounds, this section is a must for you. Chapter 4 presents a full selection of strengthening exercises for the entire body. Chapter 5 puts these exercises into effective programs that you can select from to achieve optimal, functional muscle development.

Because power is associated with how much force you produce to move from one point to another in a certain period of time, part III, "Power in Motion," presents exercises and drills to add speed, quickness, and agility to the strength you're developing from the exercises and programs in part II. It includes chapters on plyometrics, speed training, and agility training that will take you to a higher level of performance.

"Basketball Conditioning Power Rating System" (chapter 9) and "Complete Power Conditioning Program" (chapter 10) will help you monitor and fine-tune your training for maximum results. Provided in the back of the book are the anatomy muscle drawings and corresponding exercise muscle reference charts. A handy list of definitions is provided in the back of the book for easy reference if you come across a term you don't know.

Any basketball player who follows the principles and programs and who performs the exercises, drills, and workouts as instructed will be a leaner, stronger, quicker, faster, healthier, and most of all, more powerful player. Don't expect instant results but do expect success as the components of our power conditioning program begin to take effect.

We encourage you to set goals for each part of the conditioning program, based on your initial Basketball Conditioning (BC) Power Rating in each of the eight tests. Monitor your progress with testing at monthly intervals. A warning: Think long term, not short term. Athletes who try to get in shape all at once usually become disappointed or injured. Determine where you would like to be physically in one year, including your body weight, strength, speed, and BC Power Rating. If you're realistic, positive, and diligent about your power conditioning, you'll reach the goals you set.

The NBCCA wishes you great success with your conditioning and your game!

Bill Foran
President, National Basketball
Conditioning Coaches Association

A Special Note to Readers

The exercises and drills in this book follow carefully planned guidelines. By following these guidelines closely, you will obtain the best possible results. Before beginning any new exercise program, be sure to see your physician.

PART

I

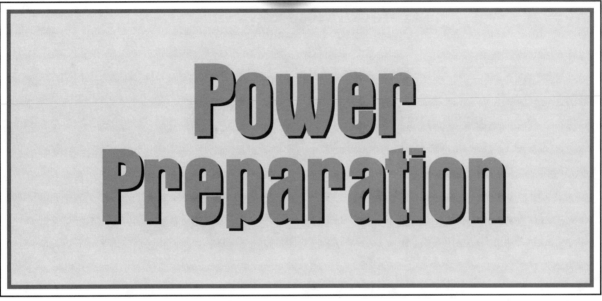

Power Preparation

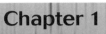

STRETCHING, WARM-UP, AND COOL-DOWN

o stretch or not to stretch? Some players and coaches ask that question, but not in NBA. Players and coaches who've made it to the highest level of the sport know and praise the benefits of stretching. Here's what some of them have to say on the subject.

"I believe the importance of stretching has been greatly overlooked in the past by some coaches and players," says Danny Ainge, head coach of the Phoenix Suns. "I have my players stretch as a team before all practices and after some selected practices throughout the season. I think stretching improves performance and reduces the chances of some injuries."

"Stretching has improved my overall agility," claims Danny Manning of the Phoenix Suns. "When I stretch before games, I feel more ready to perform, and I get into the groove easier."

Seattle SuperSonics guard Hersey Hawkins recommends stretching for players at all levels. "Flexibility has always been a big part of my game in high school, college, and now in my professional career," says Hawkins.

"When I played, a lot of players did not take stretching seriously," said Bob McAdoo, the NBA MVP in 1975 and current assistant coach of the Miami Heat. "Luckily as a rookie in 1972, my coach, Jack Ramsay, emphasized the importance of stretching. That helped me throughout my 20-year professional career."

Stretching techniques and programs have evolved in the last 25 years from something very general to something very specialized—almost a science. Perhaps the most exciting part of this evolution is that the practice of stretching is clear and simple, so that today's athlete can stretch effectively with ease. Most coaches have recognized the value of stretching and now include it as an integral part of their conditioning regimen.

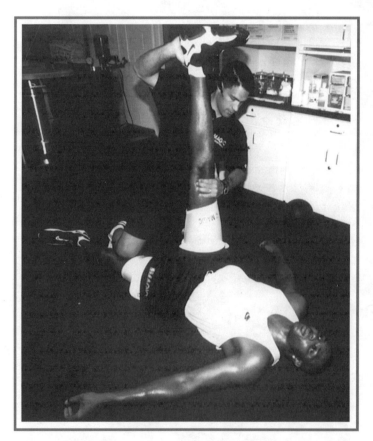

Horace Grant is being stretched by strength and conditioning coach David Oliver.

WHY STRETCHING IS IMPORTANT

The primary goal of every stretching program is to increase the range of motion (ROM) of specific joints in your body. Sufficient ROM is a key component for good health and fitness. The importance of full ROM is even more significant for athletes. Why? Because athletes' physical well-being and performance are directly related to the ability of the muscles to move through a wide range of motions. In a structured stretching program, athletes will be able to see and feel the rewards of increased flexibility in two vital areas:

- **Increased performance.** An effective stretching program will help athletes increase their power, speed, and muscle recovery time, and reduce their muscle tightness. Stretching during warm-up also helps to prepare athletes both mentally and physically for practices and games.

- **Decreased injuries.** Athletes who stretch properly have fewer strains (of muscles), sprains (of tendons), and overuse injuries. Stretching also helps diminish general muscle soreness and low-back pain and spasms.

"I have to stretch before each practice and before each and every game," says Del Curry of the Charlotte Hornets. "I can tell a big difference in how I feel and perform. I'll also stretch a lot during the off-season, before and after training, to help prevent injury."

ANATOMY AND PHYSIOLOGY OF STRETCHING

Before you take up stretching in a serious way, you need to understand a few things about how the body is constructed (anatomy) and how the body works (physiology). A basic knowledge of the human anatomy is important to you as an athlete. It will help you understand why you should stretch muscles in certain ways and not in others. In particular, you should learn a few things about joints, bones, cartilage, and ligaments.

The human body has a fascinating system of movement. All movement in our bodies revolves around our joints. The ROM of joints can either limit or enhance your body's ability to move efficiently. By increasing your joint flexibility, or ROM, you will increase your capacity to move and perform basketball skills.

At the same time, increasing your ROM means that you will decrease the chances for injuring your joints. The most effective way you can increase ROM is by regularly performing the stretching exercises presented in this chapter.

CONDITIONING TIP

When you stretch, breathe slowly and rhythmically. Exhale as you begin, then breathe slowly as you hold the stretch. Count during the stretch, saying the numbers out loud to prevent you from holding your breath. If a stretch inhibits your natural breathing pattern, ease up on the stretch so that you can breathe naturally.

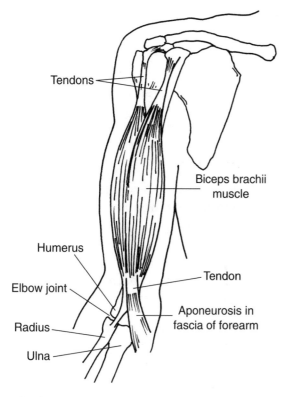

Tendons

Biceps brachii muscle

Humerus

Elbow joint

Tendon

Radius

Aponeurosis in fascia of forearm

Ulna

A body joint showing the tendons, bones, and muscles joined to form a musculotendinous unit.

From *Principles of Anatomy and Physiology,* Second Edition, by G. Tortora and N. Anagnostakos. Copyright © 1978 by Gerard J. Tortora and Nicholas P. Anagnostakos. Reprinted by permission of Addison-Wesley Educational Publishers.

To help you understand how joints move, look at how your joints are structured (see figure at left). A typical joint is composed of muscles, tendons, bones, cartilage, and ligaments. Tendons connect muscle to bone, forming what is called the musculotendinous unit.

The amazing thing about muscles is that they are elastic. Like a rubber band, muscles can stretch. Muscles can also contract or shorten. Because of their unique ability to stretch and contract, muscles allow great ROM in the joints.

Bones and cartilage provide structural support and surfaces in the joints to allow movement to occur more easily. Ligaments are the primary stabilizing tissues for bones. Ligaments connect bones to bones.

Young athletes become less flexible and sustain more injuries when they grow rapidly during adolescence. Rapid growth of muscle and bone places a great amount of stress on the joints. They become tight and pull on the bones irregularly, causing joint problems to occur. Without regular stretching, the muscles won't have a chance to maintain their flexibility.

As athletes age, their joints lose their range of motion in direct response to decreased physical activity. Stretching can stop or slow this trend of tightening up with age. NBA veteran Hersey Hawkins has a greater appreciation for stretching in the later stages of his career: "The more years I put into the league, the more I realize how important stretching is."

Muscle Properties

Muscle can shorten, or contract, and it can lengthen, or stretch. These two basic movements maintain a close working relationship. All body movements depend on this reciprocal contracting-lengthening relationship.

Whenever a muscle contracts, there is at the same time an immediate lengthening of the opposite muscle group. For example, when performing a free throw, the triceps muscle group contracts during the follow-through while the biceps muscle group lengthens, allowing for full extension at the elbow joint. You can greatly enhance your ability to perform when you condition your muscles so that they can perform at their optimum level (see the appendix for muscle diagrams and muscle charts).

As mentioned earlier, muscles are attached to bones by tendons, usually, though not always, in two places. A basic knowledge of human anatomy is important in the athlete's understanding of why muscles are stretched in different ways. A more in-depth understanding of muscle anatomy is vital for those coaches performing passive stretching on their players.

Muscle at Work

Muscles are made up of fibers. Muscle fibers have both elastic and contractile properties, which work closely together to control movement. Muscle fibers and tendons contain nerve receptors that sense any stretching or tensing in the muscles. The two nerve receptors are called muscle spindles and golgi tendon organs and are referred to as proprioceptors. They act as stretch and tension receptors to prevent injuries to muscles and tendons.

Muscles have a built-in safety mechanism, called the myotatic stretch reflex, which protects the body against extreme ROM. When muscle is stretched too quickly, it elicits the reflex response, which starts a contraction in the same muscle. By resisting any more lengthening, the reflex response protects against potential muscle strains.

This built-in safety mechanism in the muscle is the primary reason we recommend and use static stretching (holding a stretch) over ballistic stretching (bouncing). It also explains why ballistic stretching triggers this reflex and tightens rather than lengthens the muscles that are being stretched. When you stretch too far or too quickly, which often happens in ballistic stretching, you can actually tighten the muscle you are trying to stretch.

© NBA Photos/Fernando Medina

Penny Hardaway shows his explosiveness as he goes up to score.

STRETCHING TECHNIQUES

You can perform stretches in a variety of ways. Here are the four stretching techniques that we will discuss in this chapter.

Static Stretching (Individual Stretching)

Static stretches are those that are held in a fixed range of motion for a given time. You should move into all static stretches slowly until a good feeling develops. That is to say, you may feel some discomfort, but you should never feel pain.

When using static stretches

- hold each stretch 15 to 20 seconds,
- repeat each movement twice,

- stretch five to seven times each week, and
- always try to do a full-body stretch.

Dynamic Stretching

Dynamic stretches are performed through a fuller range of motion and are more aggressive than static stretches. Perform them following static stretches to prepare for practice or competition. Dynamic stretching helps stimulate the activity of the nervous system in specific joints. You're letting your muscles and joints know that you are warming them up in preparation for more vigorous activity, such as practice or competition.

> **CONDITIONING TIP**
>
> Always listen to your body. Never continue an exercise if you are experiencing pain. Pain is your body's way of telling you to stop. While stretching you should feel tension, not pain or discomfort.

Dynamic stretching has also been referred to as ballistic stretching. We feel the term *dynamic stretching* better describes the true nature of this form of stretching. The term *ballistic stretching* implies bouncing.

The goal of dynamic stretching is to increase ROM by performing sport-specific movements. Dynamic stretching is a transitional phase between static stretches and competition.

Even though dynamic stretching may not fit into the most rigid definition of stretching, it's extremely beneficial during warm-ups because it continues to increase a player's ROM. The two forms of dynamic stretching are standing drills and sport-specific speed and movement drills.

Passive Partner Stretching

Passive stretching is performed on an athlete by a partner or a coach. Proper technique is crucial to ensure safety. Passive stretching is extremely effective in gaining increased joint range of motion. The partner or coach must use caution or injury can occur.

NBA strength and conditioning coaches encourage partner stretching for the following reasons:

- Range of motion is more likely to be increased because the partner can isolate the muscle being stretched.
- The player develops a personal sense of stretching by knowing what is too much of a stretch, or too little of a stretch, while stretching a teammate.
- Players interact during the warm-up.
- Partner stretching allows the coach hands-on work with the athlete.

Either a coach or teammate may serve as a partner for passive stretches. Whoever is involved must use proper technique throughout the movement. Here are some quick tips:

- The stretcher should perform these movements slowly and with control.
- Passive stretches should not be painful; mild tension is the most the athlete should feel.
- The athlete should be stretched until he or she feels that it is a good stretch. More is not always better.
- The athlete being stretched and the stretcher (facilitator) should maintain constant oral communication to ensure that the stretch is safe and adequate.

PNF Stretching (Proprioceptive Neuromuscular Facilitation)

PNF is an advanced form of passive stretching. Strong research evidence now supports this form of stretching.

Again, the coach or partner performing this style of stretching must use extreme care. We highly recommend that the coach or facilitator be skilled in stretching techniques and have enough knowledge of PNF to ensure the safety of the athlete.

There are several preferred techniques of PNF stretching. The two techniques most commonly used by the strength and conditioning coaches of the NBA are *contract, hold, relax, movement* and *contract, movement, relax.*

STRETCHING SEQUENCE

The order in which you stretch is important. It's common to start with center-of-movement stretches, those involving the back, hips, and hamstrings. This sequence facilitates the maximum potential for full-body flexibility by first stretching the muscles that affect the rest of the body. Stretching the largest muscle groups first allows for greater potential flexibility in the smaller muscle groups.

Most movement is generated through your center of gravity (lower back and hips). The hamstrings are directly influenced by the hips and lower back. After you

> **CONDITIONING TIP**
>
> A muscle that is stretched rapidly will elicit a reflex contraction of that muscle. Do not bounce when you stretch! Bouncing will cause more harm than good.

Shawn Kemp is being stretched by strength and conditioning coach Bob Medina. Partner stretching is extremely effective in gaining increased joint range of motion.

stretch those muscle groups, you can move on to the rest of the body. We recommend the following sequence for stretching muscles over the entire body:

Torso and Lower Body

1. Back (torso)
2. Hips (pelvic region)
3. Hamstrings
4. Groin (adductors)
5. Quadriceps
6. Calves, ankles, and feet

Upper Body

1. Shoulder girdle
2. Arms, wrists, and hands
3. Neck

Use this as a general guide in sequencing your stretches. Time constraints or situational factors may force you to change the order on occasion. Just remember that stretching larger muscle groups first usually works best.

Individual Static Stretches

STANDING STRADDLE, RIGHT LEG

Muscles stretched: hamstrings, gluteals, erector spinae, and adductors

- Perform standing with feet apart in a straddle position.
- Keep knees slightly bent and toes pointed outward at a 45-degree angle.
- Bend slowly from the waist, bringing your chest toward your knee.
- Keep your back flat.
- Stretch until you feel tension in your hamstrings.

Hold 15 seconds.

Repeat twice.

STANDING STRADDLE, CENTER

Muscles stretched: hamstrings, gluteals, erector spinae, and thigh adductors

- Stand in a straddle position.
- Keep knees slightly bent and toes pointed outward at a 45-degree angle.
- Bend forward from the waist, bringing your hands toward the floor in front of you.
- Keep your back flat.
- Stretch until you feel tension in your hamstrings.

Hold 15 seconds.
Repeat twice.

STANDING STRADDLE, LEFT LEG

Muscles stretched: hamstrings, gluteals, erector spinae, and adductors

- Perform standing in a straddle position.
- Keep knees slightly bent and toes pointed outward at a 45-degree angle.
- Bend slowly from the waist, bringing your chest toward your knee.
- Keep your back flat.
- Stretch until you feel tension in your hamstrings.

Hold 15 seconds.
Repeat twice.

SIDE LUNGE

Muscles stretched: thigh adductors (groin) and hamstrings

- Start in a standing straddle position.
- Facing forward, slowly lunge to the left.
- Keep your back in a straight position and your feet at a 45-degree angle.
- Do not let your left knee move beyond your left foot.
- Point the opposite toes up toward the ceiling (into a dorsiflexed heel-down, toe-up position).

Hold 15 seconds.

- Switch legs.

Repeat exercise twice.

ILIOTIBIAL BAND STRETCH

Muscles stretched: gluteals, hamstrings, tensor fasciae latae, and erector spinae

- Start in a standing position.
- Cross your right leg over your left leg.
- Keep your knees slightly bent.
- Bend slowly, moving your hands toward the ankle of your back leg.
- Switch legs and repeat stretch.

Hold 15 seconds.
Repeat twice.

SEATED GROIN STRETCH

Muscles stretched: thigh adductors (groin)

- Sit up tall with the bottom of your feet together and knees facing outward.
- Press your knees toward the floor with your elbows.
- Stretch until you feel tension in the inner thigh (groin).

Hold 15 seconds.
Repeat twice.

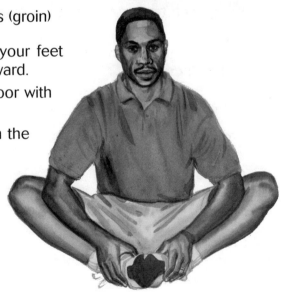

SINGLE KNEE TO CHEST STRETCH (SUPINE)

Muscles stretched: gluteals and erector spinae

- Lie on your back.
- Keep the uninvolved knee slightly bent; you may place a towel roll under your knee.
- Slowly pull your other knee toward your chest until you feel a good stretch.
- Switch legs, repeat stretch.

Hold 15 seconds.

Repeat twice.

HAMSTRING STRETCH (SUPINE)

Muscles stretched: hamstrings, gastrocnemius (calves), and some gluteals, depending on ROM

- Lie on your back.
- Bring knee to chest and slowly extend your leg.
- Point your toes (plantar flex) and contract your calf muscle.

Hold 10 seconds.

- Dorsiflex (toes pointed toward your head).

**Hold for another
10 seconds (by now you're holding for a total of 20 seconds).**

Repeat twice.

CROSSOVER STRETCH

Muscles stretched: gluteals, obliques, abdominals, tensor fasciae latae, and erector spinae

- From supine hamstring position, slowly cross your leg over and try to maintain a 90-degree position.
- Bring your foot toward your hand.

- Make sure to keep your shoulders flat on the floor during the stretch.

Hold 15 seconds.

- Switch legs.

Repeat exercise twice.

LATERAL HIP STRETCH

Muscles stretched: piriformis (deep lateral hip), gluteals, and tensor fasciae latae

- Lying on your back, cross your left leg over your right knee.
- With the ankle of your left leg, touch the right knee.
- Keep your back, shoulders, and head on the floor.

- Grab your right leg and pull it slowly until you feel your left hip being stretched.

Hold 15 seconds.

- Switch legs.

Repeat exercise twice.

PRETZEL STRETCH

Muscles stretched: erector spinae, gluteals, and abdominals

- Sitting upright, place your right hand behind you and rotate your head and shoulders toward your hand.
- Keep your left leg straight.
- Bend your right leg and cross it over your left. Push your right knee across your body with your left elbow until you feel the stretch in your right hip and torso.

Hold 15 seconds.

- Switch legs.

Repeat exercise twice.

FORWARD LUNGE

Muscles stretched: iliopsoas and rectus femoris

- In a standing position, lunge forward by placing your right foot forward.
- Make sure your knee doesn't move beyond the ball of your foot.
- Push the hip of your straight leg forward.

Hold 15 seconds.

- Switch legs.

Repeat exercise twice.

STANDING QUADRICEPS STRETCH

Muscles stretched: quadriceps, iliopsoas, and anterior tibialis

- In a standing position, balance yourself by holding on to a wall or chair.
- Grasp your right foot near the toes and pull your heel up toward your gluteal muscles.
- Push your right hip forward for a better hip flexor stretch.

Hold 15 seconds.

- Switch legs.

Repeat exercise twice.

To increase flexibility hold the stretch longer. Remember, never bounce.

STANDING CALF STRETCH

Muscles stretched: straight leg—gastrocnemius; bent leg—soleus

- In a standing, forward-lunging position, place your hands ahead of you on a wall and support yourself.
- Press the heel of your back leg toward the floor while keeping your leg straight.

Hold 15 seconds, then repeat with the knee slightly bent.
Hold 15 seconds.

- Switch legs.

Repeat exercise twice.
Be sure to stretch calves with legs straight as well as knees bent.

Standing Drills

SIDE-TO-SIDE KICK THROUGH

- Facing a wall, or holding on to a rail or fence, position your body so that you are two to three feet from the wall.
- Keep your knee slightly bent.
- Swing your right leg to the side.
- Swing your right leg across the left while swiveling your hips.
- Kick your right leg to a position where you feel a stretch in your hamstring and follow the path of the foot with your head.

Do 10 kicks.

Switch legs and repeat exercise. If you feel discomfort, reduce the height of the stretch.

FORWARD-TO-BACK KICK THROUGH

- With your right shoulder perpendicular to a wall or fence, support yourself by placing your right hand on the wall.
- Keep the knee slightly bent and maintain good posture in the back.
- Do not arch or curl your back.
- Balancing yourself with your right hand and left foot, swing your right leg up so that it is close to parallel with the floor.

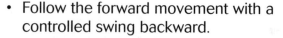

- Follow the forward movement with a controlled swing backward.
- Start with easy swings and increase the height and speed of each movement as you feel more comfortable.

Do 10 kicks.
Switch legs, repeat exercise.

Sport-Specific Movement Drills

ANKLE FLIPS

- With knees slightly bent and body in perfect alignment (shoulder, hip, knee, and ankle in a straight line), get as high on the balls of the feet as possible.
- Forcefully jump off of the balls of your feet in alternating fashion while jumping with slightly bent knees. Land on the balls of your feet, not flat-footed.
- As the right foot pushes off, the left foot should slide above the floor surface.

HIGH-KNEE MARCHING

- Alternately drive the right and left knees upward toward the chest.
- Use aggressive arm movements. Bend the arm of the straight leg and swing the opposite arm behind you.
- As you march keep the raised foot dorsiflexed (heel-down, toe-up position).
- Be sure to land on your toes, not flat footed.

March 10 to 30 yards.
Repeat.

HIGH-KNEE WITH LEG REACH

- Alternately drive the right and left knees upward toward the chest.
- When the knee is in the up position, extend the leg.

- With the right leg extended, finish the movement by aggressively extending the thigh downward at the hip.
- Follow this movement with the opposite leg.

March 20 to 30 yards.

Repeat.

HEEL KICKS

- While running forward aggressively, flex your legs at the knees.
- Try to touch your gluteals with your heels.
- Keep your thigh perpendicular to the running surface. Point your toes as your heel moves toward the gluteals.

Move forward 20 yards.
Repeat.

CARIOCA

- Moving laterally, swivel your hips so that your right leg crosses in front of the left.
- Step to the side with left leg.
- Cross right leg behind left leg.

Move quickly for 30 yards.
Repeat.

- Switch direction and lead with opposite leg.

Repeat exercise.

BACKWARD STRIDE

- Run backward by alternately reaching back with each foot.
- Use an extended stride.

Run 30 yards.
Repeat.

Passive Partner Stretching

During the stretching phase of the warm-up, begin the partner-stretching program with low back (torso) and hamstring stretches.

SEATED STRADDLE

Muscles stretched: hamstrings, thigh adductors, gluteals, and erector spinae

- Player sits in a straddle position (V-sit).
- Partner applies pressure with the hands—slowly and evenly—to the player's low to midback.
- Player should bend from the hips, keeping the back flat.
- This stretch should be performed to the right, middle, and left sides.

DOUBLE KNEE TO CHEST

Muscles stretched: gluteals and erector spinae

- Player lies on back with both knees bent.
- Partner places hands on hamstrings or bottom of feet and applies pressure downward to take knees into chest.

Perform for 20 seconds.
Repeat.

SINGLE KNEE TO CHEST

Muscles stretched: gluteals and erector spinae

- Player lies on back with one knee bent and the foot raised.
- The partner presses the bottom of the player's foot toward the player's hip, bringing the knee to the chest.
- Partner places one hand at the bottom of the foot and the other on the knee that's on the ground.

Perform for 20 seconds.
Repeat on opposite side.
Repeat exercise.

KNEE ACROSS BODY

Muscles stretched: gluteals, tensor fasciae latae, abdominals, and erector spinae

- Go directly into this stretch by taking the raised single knee to the chest across the opposite side of the body, keeping both shoulder blades on the floor.

Perform twice for 20 seconds with each knee.

Repeat single knee to chest and knee across body stretches with the other leg.

LYING HAMSTRING STRETCH

Muscles stretched: hamstrings, gastrocnemius (calves), and some gluteals, depending on ROM

- Player lies on the floor.
- While the left leg is straight, partner takes right heel of player and elevates leg to stretch hamstring.

Perform twice, holding each time for 20 seconds.

Repeat on the other leg.

PIRIFORMIS STRETCH

Muscles stretched: piriformis and gluteals

- Player, lying on back with both knees bent, takes right ankle and crosses it over on top of left knee.
- Partner places both hands on top of player's left knee and applies pressure to move player's left knee and right ankle toward chest.

Perform twice, holding each time for 20 seconds.

Repeat with left ankle across right knee.

I.T. BAND STRETCH (CROSSOVER)

Muscles stretched: tensor fasciae latae, gluteals, and hamstrings

- Player lies on back with shoulder blades flat on floor.
- Partner slowly takes the player's right leg and crosses it over the other.
- Keep the opposite leg in place.
- The legs should be positioned at approximately 90 degrees when the right leg is crossed over the left.

Perform twice, holding each time for 20 seconds.

Repeat on the other leg.

BUTTERFLY STRETCH

Muscles stretched: thigh adductors

- Player lies on back with both knees bent, soles of feet together.
- Partner applies pressure on top of bent knees downward toward floor.

Perform twice, holding each time for 20 seconds.

QUADRICEPS STRETCH (SINGLE LEG)

Muscles stretched: quadriceps, iliopsoas, and rectus femoris

- Player lies on the floor, face down with left leg bent and right leg straight.
- Slowly the partner lifts the player's left knee.
- Partner should put the right hand on the player's gluteals.

Perform twice, holding each time for 20 seconds.

Repeat on the other leg.

CHEST STRETCH

Muscles stretched: pectorals and anterior deltoids

- Player—sitting, standing, or kneeling—places both hands behind head.
- Partner, from behind, places both bent elbows into his or her hands and applies pressure by pulling elbows backward, behind the player's head.

Perform twice, holding each time for 20 seconds.

SHOULDER AND BICEPS STRETCH

Muscles stretched: biceps, anterior deltoids, and pectorals

- Player sits, kneels, or stands.
- Partner takes both wrists into hands, palms facing up, and elevates the straight arms until the player feels the stretch.

Perform twice, holding each time for 20 seconds.

PNF Stretching

PNF (proprioceptive neuromuscular facilitation) is an advanced form of passive stretching.

Use caution when applying this technique.

The two PNF techniques most commonly used by NBA strength and conditioning coaches are *contract, hold, relax, movement* and *contract, movement, relax*. Following are examples of both techniques.

Hamstring Stretch: Contract, Hold, Relax, Movement

Procedure: Athlete isometrically contracts the hamstring muscles while the coach pushes against the athlete's resistance. The player holds this isometric contraction for 5 to 10 seconds and then relaxes for 10 seconds. After this hold, the athlete is stretched further. Repeat three times.

Partner tip: It is vital that the partner talks to the athlete. During the exercise, the partner might say to the athlete, "Contract against my hold." Following the stretch, the partner should give the command, "OK, now relax."

Hamstring Stretch: Contract, Movement, Relax

Procedure: This stretch is performed in a manner similar to the contract, hold, relax technique. Here the athlete attempts to push his or her leg toward the partner by contracting the hamstring muscles. The partner allows the leg to move in a predetermined range of motion before giving the "relax" command. During the relaxation phase, the partner moves the leg into a deeper stretched position and repeats. Repeat cycle three times.

WARM-UP

Proper warm-up is essential in preparing an athlete for practice or competition. Every warm-up session should include a stretching portion with both static and dynamic stretching. A complete basketball warm-up takes 20 to 30 minutes and has three phases.

The first phase is the general warm-up, during which the athlete will elevate the body core temperature by performing physical activities such as light jogging, easy rope jumping, or calisthenic-type exercises. The athlete should perform these activities for 5 to 10 minutes or until sweating begins.

The second phase calls for the athlete to perform a passive, full-body stretching routine that involves all the major muscle groups. This phase takes 10 to 12 minutes.

The final part of the warm-up includes dynamic stretching, form running (multidirectional), standing drills, and sport-specific movement drills. After 5 to 7 minutes of these activities, the athlete should be fully prepared for the physical demands that follow in practice or games.

THREE PHASES OF WARM-UP

1. General warm-up
   - Jog forward or backward, shuffle, and carioca (3 minutes)
   - Jump rope: (1) double leg, (2) right leg, (3) left leg, (4) double leg (5 minutes)
2. Passive, static stretching
   - Full-body stretch (12 minutes)
3. Sport-specific warm-up and dynamic stretching
   - Standing drills: kick throughs left and right (two sets of 15 reps, each leg)
   - Movement drills: marching, high-knee skipping, heel kicks, backward running, and forward strides (two sets of 20 yards, each drill)

COOL-DOWN

While a warm-up helps get you ready for practice and games, the cool-down afterward is important for muscle recovery and returning the body to its resting state. Cooling down involves a period of light exercise for 5 to 10 minutes following workouts. We also recommend stretching of the low back, hamstrings, quadriceps, and other muscle groups.

Many NBA teams include postpractice cool-down sessions as a part of their daily routines for two reasons:

- A cool-down helps muscles recover faster and may reduce the potential for muscle cramping and injuries during future workouts. Continued circulation provided by the cool-down process allows the body to restore proper fluid, electrolyte, enzyme, and nutrient balance in the muscle cells. This is especially important during two-a-day sessions.

- The cool-down helps convert the acids found in the blood and working muscles that were created during the vigorous workout back to preexercise (normal) levels. Continued circulation provided by the cool-down aids in delivering oxygen and various nutrients to the blood and muscles, helping to remove waste products and restore energy back to your system.

CONDITIONING TIP

Stretching is an essential part of warm-up, but it can be especially effective following practice during the cool-down because muscles are warm and are capable of greater ROM. To avoid risk of injury always stretch before and after a workout.

Sports like basketball that are anaerobic in nature produce lactate in blood and muscle as a product of the high-intensity work. So it's in your best interest to do what the pros do, that is, stay healthy by performing both a warm-up and a cool-down.

A typical cool-down might include the following sequence of activities:

1. Light jog (3 minutes)
2. Abdominal work (3 minutes)
3. Free-throw shooting (5 to 10 minutes)
4. Stretching (5 to 10 minutes)

This is only one example. The important thing is to develop a cool-down routine that meets your needs and then make time for it in your conditioning program.

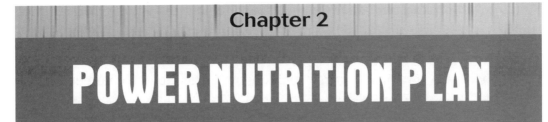

POWER NUTRITION PLAN

ou are what you eat." You probably heard those words a hundred times from your parents while you were growing up. In this chapter you'll hear, "You perform like you eat," because eating right is important if you want to excel on the court.

The foods you consume serve as fuel for your body. So, what you eat affects the way you play and how effectively you train. If you eat food low in nutritional value, your performance and conditioning results won't be what they could have been.

Champion thoroughbreds and winning racing cars are fed optimum fuels. Their high-quality diets allow them to perform to their highest potential. You can work out from sunup to sundown, but unless you fill yourself with the right nutrients, you'll fail to reach your basketball performance potential. In addition, your body will not recover as quickly after an exhausting game or workout.

FOOD ENERGY REQUIREMENTS FOR BASKETBALL

Food is energy or fuel for your body. The harder you work your body, the more fuel or calories you'll burn. The average daily energy requirements of athletes vary according to body weight, body composition, age, sex, and activity level (see table 2-1).

Basketball players require many calories, from the right food sources, to reach and maintain a high conditioning level. And through year-round conditioning, players can avoid a calorie surplus—gaining fat weight—during the off-season.

Table 2-1 Calories Burned In Different Sports			
Activity	Calories burned per hour	Activity	Calories burned per hour
Bicycling	204	Football (touch)	476
Swimming	299	Aerobics (heavy)	544
Walking	299	Racquetball	544
Volleyball	345	Skiing	598
Ice skating	394	Weight-lifting (heavy)	612
Tennis	414	**Basketball**	**680**
Jogging	476	Running	897

Table 2-2 indicates the daily calorie intake guidelines for athletes. Remember, if you're training hard for basketball, base your calorie needs on the higher numbers.

Let's say you're a 17-year-old male weighing 180 pounds. Because of your sex, age, size, and intense basketball training, you'll need nearly 4,000 calories a day to provide the required energy (180 × 22 = 3,960 calories).

Table 2-2 Daily Energy Recommendations for Athletes		
	CALORIES NEEDED PER POUND OF WEIGHT	
Age	**Male**	**Female**
11 - 14	24 - 28	20 - 24
15 - 18	18 - 22	16 - 20
19 - 22	18 - 22	16 - 20

NUTRITION BASICS

Every athlete should eat a well-balanced diet. That starts with plenty of fluids in the form of water and juices and the proper mix of carbohydrate, protein, and fat. Sport nutritionists generally recommend a diet with the following energy-nutrient breakdown:

- 60 to 65 percent carbohydrates
- 15 to 20 percent proteins
- 20 to 25 percent fats

These three nutrients contain different amounts of calories. Carbohydrates and proteins each have 4 calories per gram. Fats, however, have 9 calories per gram. Just one serving of a food containing 11 grams of fat has 99 calories, whereas 11 grams of carbohydrate has only 44 calories! Because fats are more than twice as calorie dense as either carbohydrates or proteins, an athlete trying to lose weight should reduce fat intake to minimum required levels and increase carbohydrate intake.

Your body uses carbohydrates as its primary source of fuel during most of your physical activity in workouts, practices, and games. During longer athletic activity, your body begins using fats as energy. And when nothing else is left, the body starts feeding on protein to keep it going.

The Six Classes of Nutrients

There are six classes of nutrients: water, carbohydrates, proteins, fats, vitamins, and minerals.

Water

Water is the most critical element in your diet. Under moderate exercise and weather conditions, you need about two quarts of water per day. Your body needs all this water to digest and absorb food, and to excrete waste. Water also helps maintain blood plasma levels and lubricate organs and joints. You can go a long time without food, but you won't survive long without water.

Water plays two important roles when you exercise. For one, it regulates your body temperature, keeping you cool during workouts. It also transports nutrients and by-products into and out of cells.

Follow these guidelines to make sure you're getting enough water:

- Drink six to eight glasses of water each day.
- Drink two glasses of water 15 minutes before workouts or competition.
- Drink two glasses of water beyond thirst requirements after workouts or competitions.
- Drink one glass of water every 15 to 30 minutes during workouts or competitions.
- Drink chilled liquids to speed absorption from the stomach into the blood and to cool off the body faster.
- Drink one glass of water after consuming caffeinated drinks within 12 hours of workouts. Caffeine is a diuretic, which means it will cause dehydration.

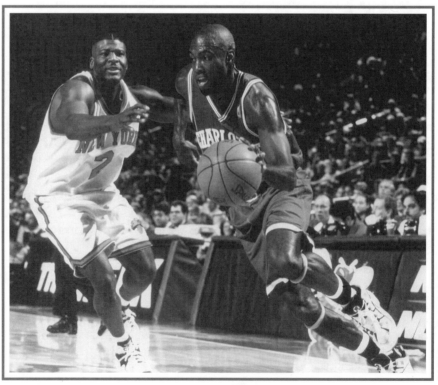

© NBA Photos/Nathaniel S. Butler

All basketball players, including Glen Rice lose a lot of water through sweating while playing during games. Competitors need to drink water every 15 to 30 minutes while playing to keep from dehydrating.

Humans have an inaccurate thirst mechanism. We aren't thirsty until long after we've run a water deficit. Therefore, you'll have to train yourself to drink water regularly, especially when you're working out or playing. The experts call it hydration, and it's essential for your health and conditioning.

Carbohydrates

Carbohydrates, composed of sugars and starches, have two forms: simple and complex. Simple carbohydrates consist of some fruits, juices, soft drinks, and sweets. Complex carbohydrates include whole grains, pasta, rice, breads, and vegetables.

As the name suggests, a carbohydrate is a substance that's made up of carbon and hydrogen atoms, which give a person energy. The carbohydrate you probably know best is sugar. Sugar is the carbohydrate that fuels the body.

But consuming lots of soft drinks and desserts is not the way to get good carbohydrates into your diet. Although these drinks and desserts contain plenty of sugar, that sugar is simple sugar. Simple sugars come from junk food and have no nutritional value. Simple sugars are foods that lack nutrients, vitamins, and minerals; they contain empty calories. They provide quick energy but only for a brief time. Simple sugars won't give you enough energy to get through practice, let alone the second half of a game.

Much better sources of energy are complex carbohydrates, also referred to as complex sugars. The body breaks down complex carbohydrates into glucose and stores it in muscle tissue and the liver as glycogen. Your body needs glucose for your muscles to work effectively.

Knowing which foods contain simple sugars and which contain complex sugars is the key to fueling your body with the best source of energy. Complex carbohydrates include some fruits, vegetables, breads, pasta, and potatoes.

Complex carbohydrates contain nutrients, vitamins, and minerals. And because complex carbohydrates are nutritionally dense, you can eat larger quantities without adding up empty calories. Complex carbohydrates will also give you a more satisfied, fuller feeling for a longer time. As a result, you won't feel that you need to snack on junk food for a sugar fix to keep you going.

Proteins

Protein, a crucial component of healthy nutrition, is the substance that builds muscles. An athlete's muscle tissue is approximately 70 to 75 percent water and 10 to 25 percent protein. A diet that has 15 to 20 percent protein will meet the needs of nearly all athletes.

Try to get about 1 to 1.5 grams of protein per kilogram (2.2 pounds) of your body weight each day. If you're 176 pounds, that's about 80 grams of protein per day. You could meet this requirement with three glasses of milk, two medium-sized chicken breasts, and a slice of cheese or the equivalent. Good sources of protein include beef, pork, poultry, fish, eggs, and dairy products. Once you've met your protein requirement, the extra protein is converted to and stored as fat or is excreted from your body.

Eating large amounts of protein won't make you bigger, faster, or stronger. Proper conditioning develops those attributes. Actually, protein is a poor source of energy. It's much better to obtain your energy supply from complex carbohydrates.

Proteins are a combination of smaller units called amino acids. Twenty-two known amino acids are required to support growth and development. Your body can manufacture 13 of them; your diet must provide the other 9, which are considered "essential amino acids." A food that contains all essential amino acids is a complete protein. Vegetables are incomplete proteins because they lack essential amino acids and must be eaten in certain combinations to make a complete protein. For proper nutrition, include all the essential amino acids in your diet.

Fats

Despite their reputation, fats contribute to a well-balanced diet. Fats are known as lipids or oils and are made up of triglycerides.

A sufficient amount of fat in the diet is necessary to promote the absorption of fat-soluble vitamins such as A, D, E, and K. Most of the body's cells use fat in their makeup. Fat also insulates the body and cushions the internal organs.

If your diet includes 20 to 25 percent fat, that's enough. There is no need to add fatty foods to your diet. The health hazards of high levels of fat accumulation are well known. Even if you can burn off most of the fat you take in, we do not recommend using fat as a major source of calories or energy.

Fatty foods are hard to resist because they are so flavorful. Meat, ice cream, chocolate, whole milk, cheeses, and butter contain plenty of fat. Even "reduced-calorie" margarine contains mostly fat calories. Your body will store fatty foods that you fail to burn up as fat.

Vitamins

Your body needs vitamins, but in small quantities. Vitamins help your body perform specific functions essential for proper muscle and nerve functioning. Vitamins also release energy from foods and promote the normal growth of body tissues.

But understand that vitamins are not a *source* of energy. Some mis-

© NBA Photos/Bill Baptist

The energy shown by Mitch Richmond while running down the court comes in part from eating a well-balanced diet.

guided athletes take extra vitamins instead of eating to try to get a boost of energy. Unfortunately, all they may end up with are stomach cramps.

Vitamins are classified as either fat soluble (vitamins A, D, E and K) or water soluble (vitamins Bs and C). Water-soluble vitamins aren't stored in the body when you take them in large quantities. Excess fat-soluble vitamins are retained in the body's fat. This situation can be dangerous and lead to a condition known as hypervitaminosis—a buildup of toxic levels in the body.

Minerals

Minerals are inorganic substances that regulate bodily processes, maintain bodily tissues, and aid metabolism. Calcium, iodine, iron, phosphorus, magnesium, sodium, and potassium are a few of the body's key minerals. These minerals are also called electrolytes. Electrolytes are critical in helping working muscles maintain their normal contractions over a long period.

There are more than 20 mineral elements in the body. Of these, 17 are essential to your diet. Minerals are grouped in two classes—major (macro) minerals, which are needed in amounts greater than 100 milligrams per day; and trace (micro) minerals, which are needed only in very small amounts.

Athletes who need more vitamins and minerals can get them through supplements in tablet form. The easiest way to do this is to take a children's chewable tablet daily. Chewing ensures a greater rate of absorption into your body and helps you control the dosage. Although children's supplements aren't as potent as adults', by using them you'll reduce the amount of waste resulting from excess intake and save a little money.

The following lists shows the benefits of vitamins and minerals.

> **CONDITIONING TIP**
>
> Sodium or salt is everywhere because it's such an effective preservative. It's in about every food you buy, especially at fast-food restaurants. So, forget the salt shaker, and keep your salt intake within recommended limits.

Fat Soluble Vitamins

Vitamin A	Maintains eye and skin health Aids resistance to infection
Vitamin D	Aids absorption of calcium
Vitamin E	Protects vitamins and essential fatty acids from destruction
Vitamin K	Needed for blood clotting

Water Soluble Vitamins

Vitamin C	Strengthens body cells Promotes healing of wounds and bones Increases resistance to infection
Vitamin B2 (Riboflavin)	Used in energy metabolism Promotes good vision and healthy skin
Niacin	Used in fat and carbohydrate metabolism Promotes healthy skin, nerves, and digestive tract
Vitamin B6	Used in protein and fat metabolism Needed for red blood cell formation

Folic Acid	Used in protein metabolism
	Promotes red blood cell formation
Vitamin B12	Used in red blood cell development and in maintenance of nerve tissue

Minerals

Calcium	Used to form bones and teeth
	Helps control blood clotting as well as contracting and relaxing muscles
Iodine	Helps regulate the rate at which your body uses energy
Iron	An important part of hemoglobin, which carries oxygen throughout your body
Magnesium	Helps regulate the use of carbohydrates and the production of energy within your cells
Phosphorus	Combines with calcium to give bones and teeth strength and hardness
Potassium	Regulates the amount of water in your cells
	Is essential for proper function of the kidneys, heart, and muscles
Sodium	Regulates the amount of water in your cells
	Is essential for proper transmission of nerve impulses and contraction of the muscles
Zinc	Becomes part of several enzymes that affect cell growth and repair
	Is part of insulin, which binds with glucose to carry it through the cell membrane so it can be used as energy

Supplements

Today's supplements include drinks, powders, nutritional bars, and tablets. Some are good. Some are bad. None will make you an all-star.

Never rely on supplements for your basic nutritional needs. The body is a 24-hour-a-day processing operation, and once the supplements you've taken have moved through your system, your body will have no fuel for energy unless it has a solid nutritional base in reserve. That's why it's so important to learn to eat well. When you eat nutritionally, your body gets a continuous supply of calories, proteins, vitamins, minerals, and everything else it needs.

In deciding whether to supplement your diet, consider how doing so will fit within your daily nutritional requirements for calories, proteins, carbohydrates, and fat. Before starting down the supplement trail, ask a knowledgeable nutritionist, coach, or sports medicine professional for guidance.

If you decide to take supplements, learn the difference between what they claim to do and what they actually do. For example, powder supplements and nutritional bars will provide more calories and supply additional nutrients, such as vitamins, minerals, carbohydrates, and proteins.

Tablets are another option. If you eat well and take a powder supplement, you would probably never need more than a multivitamin or a mineral tablet to round out your nutritional intake. Research has shown that vitamins A, C, and E can serve as antioxidants and help control "free radicals" in the body, which can cause cellular damage. Smart supplementation in proper dosages and in conjunction with a balanced diet can improve your health, prevent illness, and may speed recovery from exercise.

Use a product with a proper ratio of carbohydrates, proteins, and fats. If you use a powder supplement, it should mix easily and thoroughly with water. Drink the supplement 45 to 60 minutes before or after a workout. After is your best choice. A supplement can help you add calories to your diet and assist in your recovery. But don't make supplements the focus of your nutritional program.

Sports Nutrition Guidelines

If you want to be your physical best, then learning how to eat is a critical step. The U.S. government now requires food manufacturers to list the nutritional makeup of foods on the label. Get in the practice of knowing what you're eating and learn how to eat nutritionally. Refer to chapter 10 in Nancy Clark's *Sports Nutrition Guidebook* for information on fast food and its nutritional content.

The four basic food groups were once the guide for proper nutrition. This formula has been replaced with the USDA food guide pyramid. This pyramid, shown below, is more detailed and accurate, including recommended daily servings for the different food groups.

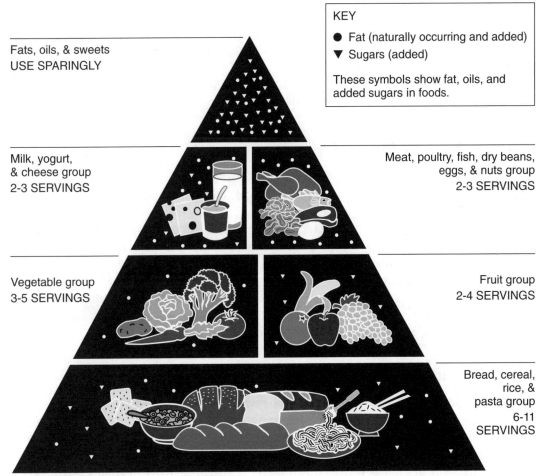

Fats, oils, & sweets
USE SPARINGLY

KEY
● Fat (naturally occurring and added)
▼ Sugars (added)

These symbols show fat, oils, and added sugars in foods.

Milk, yogurt, & cheese group
2-3 SERVINGS

Meat, poultry, fish, dry beans, eggs, & nuts group
2-3 SERVINGS

Vegetable group
3-5 SERVINGS

Fruit group
2-4 SERVINGS

Bread, cereal, rice, & pasta group
6-11 SERVINGS

United States Departments of Agriculture and Health and Human Services

The Food Guide Pyramid shows the different food groups and the number of servings recommended for each. No one food group is more important than another—for good health you need them all.

SAMPLE MEAL PLAN

To help you get the daily nutrition you need to excel on the court, here is a sample meal plan to follow:

Breakfast—a nutritional shake with fruit and low-fat milk, cereal (shredded wheat or similar), toast or bagel; during the morning, drink two or three glasses of water.

Midmorning—a sandwich is sufficient. Or you might prefer yogurt, fruit, bagels, low-fat cookies, Fig Newtons, graham crackers, Vanilla Wafers, or a sports bar (watch the sugar content).

Lunch—pasta, salad bar, grilled chicken, baked potato, sandwich (tuna, turkey, or chicken), or Chinese food (not fried, and ask for "no MSG").

Midafternoon—more water.

After workout—repeat either the breakfast or the midmorning snack.

Dinner—same approach as lunch.

Evening snack—cookies, cereal, yogurt, or a little fruit.

You may be surprised to see cereal and cookies listed here. These can be good low- or no-fat choices if you select carefully from your grocer's cookie shelf. Avoid snacking on chips; even the so-called low-fat variety contain too much fat. If you need a chip fix, opt for a few baked tortilla chips with salsa. They make a great low-calorie snack!

As indicated in our sample daily meal plan above, we believe in the principle of increasing the frequency of meals. This means that you'll eat smaller meals more often throughout the day. This is the best method to fulfill the daily nutritional needs of high-performance athletes who need to take in a large amount of calories. It's also the most efficient method for weight control, if that becomes one of your chosen goals. A Fastbreak chart with samples of foods and their nutritional makeup is included in the appendix along with a Food Record chart used to map how many calories and grams of carbohydrates, proteins, and fats you eat each day.

Pregame and Halftime

The digestion and absorption time of your food, the gastric emptying rate, takes one to four hours depending on the amounts and types of food in the meal and your activity level afterward. Fats and proteins generally take three to four hours to digest. Carbohydrates take one to three hours. To be safe, eat your pregame meal three to four hours before competition to ensure that most of the meal is out of your stomach when the action starts.

Food in your stomach causes your gastrointestinal tract and working muscles to compete for blood flow. This leads to inefficient functioning of both the GI tract and the muscles, and may also cause indigestion, cramping, nausea, and vomiting.

Your pregame meal should follow the high carbohydrate (60-65 percent), low fat (20-25 percent), and proper protein (15-20 percent) guidelines presented for your daily diet. Be sure to drink plenty of water or fruit juice with your pregame meal and throughout the day.

At halftime keep taking in fluids. Avoid drinks or any foods with too much sugar. It doesn't take much to put sugar into your blood. Be conservative. Get to know how your body responds to different drinks and snacks at the half before trying anything in large amounts. If you feel hungry, eat only half of something like a sports bar or piece of fruit. Never experiment with some new super-energy formula at halftime. Stick with what you know is safe and works for you.

A BALANCED APPROACH TO WEIGHT CONTROL

Our goal is to provide you with a long-term, flexible, balanced, and winning nutritional program. Once you know the basics, you can make the right choices and avoid irresponsible fad diets to lose or gain weight.

An optimal weight is one that will allow you to be your strongest and fastest and is easy to carry. If you are unsatisfied with your body weight, we encourage you to first determine your body composition. By body composition, we mean the amount of lean body mass (muscle) you have in contrast to your total body fat. When you know these figures, you can calculate your percentage body fat.

An elite male basketball player should have 6 to 8 percent or less body fat; an elite female basketball player should have between 12 and 15 percent body fat. If you are a male with over 15 percent body fat or a female with over 20 percent body fat, then you need to reevaluate your nutritional program.

Fat-Loss Program

Some athletes believe that being involved in a workout program gives them a blank check to eat as much as they want. If you need to drop a few pounds, then do so sensibly. That means working at it, patiently, on a daily basis. You're better off losing at the rate of three to five pounds per week (maximum) than trying a fad diet that leaves you feeling weak and is likely to fail. Insufficient nutrition can lead to a dangerous chain reaction in all systems of the body. Some things to watch for include:

- If you start to notice an increase around your middle, then something is out of line somewhere.
- If you put on weight that you think is good, but you run slower or feel more sluggish, then it is probably unwanted weight.
- If you lose weight that you think is good, but you have a significant drop in strength levels, then you may be losing muscle rather than fat.

If you want to lose or gain weight, plan to do so over a reasonable amount of time (that means weeks or months). Don't try to lose or gain a lot of weight in a short period of time. It may affect your health in negative ways.

How to Lose Fat Weight

Starvation diets are no way to lose weight. All you'll lose is water, muscle mass, and energy. Instead, follow these four key points for effective weight loss.

- Eat sensibly. Take in fewer calories by concentrating on smaller meals and eating complex carbohydrates. Don't skip meals.
- Perform at least 20 minutes of daily aerobic exercise at moderate to high intensity.
- Try cross training. You can ride a cycle, walk, jog, or use a stair-climbing machine. Try a variety of activities to keep workouts interesting.
- When it comes time to eat, choose low-fat, high-carbohydrate foods with no simple sugars (like those found in junk food), and moderate amounts of protein.

Don't make the common dieter's mistake of limiting calories and neglecting the essentials. Some athletes, for example, reduce their protein intake drastically and start losing muscle mass. Then they incorrectly assume that they are losing unwanted fat but can't figure out why they feel so weak.

"IN BOUNDS" NUTRITION TIPS

- Eat low-fat, high-fiber foods.
- Eat four to six modestly sized meals a day rather than three huge meals.
- Eat a well-balanced breakfast.
- Eat broiled foods instead of fried foods. If you can't resist fried foods, at least peel the skin off the chicken and remove the breading from vegetables.
- Snack on fresh fruit and complex carbohydrates instead of sweets or fats. Don't eat sugar or sweets after 6 PM—they suppress the growth hormone released while sleeping at night that repairs your body from daily stresses.
- Drink plenty of water.
- Avoid alcohol. Alcohol is a drug that interferes with the digestion and absorption of nutrients, suppresses the release of the growth hormone, and harms your body in many ways.
- Be careful to avoid high-fat and high-sodium selections at fast-food restaurants.
- When you dine at salad bars, eat a "rainbow" of foods. The variety of colors will help you obtain the best balance of nutrients from the foods available.
- Ask that dressings and sauces be placed on the side to control your fat intake.

Your goal should be to shed fat and add muscle. If you lose six pounds of fat and gain five pounds of muscle, the scale will show only a one-pound loss. What's important is that you have improved your body composition significantly.

Be patient with your weight loss. Remember that with proper conditioning, it's possible to lose fat and put on muscle. A pound of fat and a pound of muscle weigh the same, but that pound of fat takes up more room than the muscle. Your weight may change very little when you follow this program, but your clothes will fit you much better, and you will feel and perform better.

Weight-Gain Program

Many young athletes want to gain weight and become more powerful on the court. The key in gaining weight is to build bigger, stronger muscles, not just add pounds to your midsection.

The success of any weight-gain program hinges on these three factors:

- Diet
- Strength training
- Heredity

Diet

To gain weight you must take in more calories than your body burns. That is, you need to eat more food. You can increase your calorie intake by eating larger portions at meals, eating more meals each day, and eating snacks between meals. If you have a difficult time gaining weight, you may need to reduce your activity level to give your body enough time to rest and build.

A pound of body weight equals 3,500 calories. If you want to gain weight, you need to eat 3,500 calories more than your body uses. You can gain about one pound in a week by eating an extra 500 calories each day.

CONDITIONING TIP

Steroids may increase muscle growth and strength, but they can severely injure the functioning of your internal organs, or even kill you. They can also change your personality for the worse. Too many athletes have already suffered and died from using steroids. Use the natural conditioning methods presented in this book instead of cheating with drugs like steroids.

Strength Training

You must combine your increased calorie intake with a proper resistance or strength-training program to gain muscle mass. If you increase your calorie intake and don't exercise or lift weights, you will gain fat, not muscle. An effective strength-training program is provided in chapter 5.

Heredity

Genetic potential is the third factor in gaining weight. Some athletes gain weight at a faster rate than others. If you gain weight slowly or simply have a tough time putting on more pounds, don't become discouraged. Continue with your plan each day and good things will happen.

POWER CONDITIONING BASE

ach chapter of this book will help make you a more highly conditioned basketball player, but it all starts with a proper conditioning base. The same is true in developing high-level basketball skills; first you must learn and develop the fundamentals.

Conditioning provides an opportunity to improve yourself as an athlete and basketball player. As a better-conditioned athlete, you can perform at higher intensities and sustain efforts longer than someone who is not as well conditioned. Superior conditioning gives you a chance to reach your potential on the court and gives you an advantage over lesser-conditioned opponents.

Seattle SuperSonics guard Gary Payton is a perfect example. After an outstanding college career at Oregon State, Gary was the second player taken in the 1990 draft. Expectations of him were high. But in his first two years in the league, Gary was somewhat of a disappointment. Something was missing. In the summer of 1992, Gary knew he was at a fork in the road of his NBA career. He could stay in the league and be an average player, perhaps coming off the bench. Or he could work to improve and perhaps become one of the league's best players.

© NBA Photos/Andrew D. Bernstein

During the off-season between his second and third years in the league, Gary dedicated himself to an intense conditioning program. That season (1993) he led the SuperSonics to the NBA Western Conference Finals. His commitment to conditioning continued into 1994. He became an all-star and led his team to the best record in the NBA (63-19). Then, in 1996, Gary again demonstrated the benefits of his high-level fitness, as he led the Sonics to the NBA Finals and was named the NBA's Defensive Player of the Year.

Guard Gary Payton's dedication to conditioning has made him one of the best players in the NBA.

ENERGY SYSTEMS

Reaching a top conditioning level like that achieved by Gary Payton and other NBA stars isn't easy. It takes work. And that takes energy. Fortunately, the body has three energy systems to call upon during exercise:

- ATP-CP system
- Glycogen lactic acid system
- Aerobic system

The ATP-CP system and the glycogen lactic acid systems are anaerobic. Basketball requires repeated short-duration, high-intensity efforts that use these anaerobic systems much more than they do the aerobic system used for long-duration, low-intensity efforts.

Each energy system works more effectively at a particular period of exercise. The figure below shows that the three energy systems kick in at various time and distance exercise intervals. The connecting arrows between the three systems represent transition phases from one system to another. Note that one system does not shut off and another take over but that they work together during different periods. Only the extreme ends on the continuum represent 100 percent anaerobic or aerobic energy demands.

Primary Energy Systems

		ATP-CP			
		Glycogen lactic acid			
ATP-CP ⟷ Glycogen lactic acid	⟷ Aerobic	⟷ Aerobic			

Time:	10 seconds	1 minute	2 minutes	4 minutes	9 minutes	30 minutes	2 hours+
Distance:	100 yards	440 yards	880 yards	1 mile	2 miles	6 miles	Marathon

RECOVERY

Because basketball is a game of brief but intense and repeated bursts of action with very short rest periods in between, the ability to recover quickly is critical for players. Every player becomes tired at times during taxing practices and games, but well-conditioned athletes recover more quickly and are able to maintain their high-intensity efforts longer. By using proper rest intervals during conditioning sessions, you can develop your recovery system.

Short-Term Recovery

For well-conditioned athletes, the ATP-CP energy system recovers halfway in about 20 to 30 seconds, approximately the rest period of a 20-second time-out or a foul call and free-throw attempt. This system recovers fully in 2 to 5 minutes, roughly the length of full time-outs, quarter breaks, and short stints on the bench.

The glycogen lactic acid system recovers halfway in 20 to 30 minutes and recovers fully in one hour or more.

Long-Term Recovery

Long-term recovery takes from two days to several days depending on the extent of nutrient depletion, enzyme depletion, and tissue breakdown. A good diet, proper rest, and a quality training program accelerate recovery, repair, and replenishment.

Carbohydrates are the primary energy source used in the ATP-CP and glycogen lactic acid systems. For a more detailed discussion on nutrition see chapter 2.

OFF-SEASON CONDITIONING

The off-season is the time to prepare yourself physically for the demands of a long, intense season. The basketball conditioning program should begin 12 weeks before the first official day of preseason practice.

The program starts with 400-meter strides on a track and ends with sprints on the court. Two workouts are scheduled per week and should coincide with two days per week of plyometric and agility workouts, which also will improve your conditioning and performance level.

If you play in summer basketball leagues or play other sports, you may need to cut back a little in your conditioning or you will be susceptible to overtraining. Signs of overtraining are a feeling of weakness in the weight room, not running as well on the track, or feeling run down and fatigued. You can cut back your conditioning program by doing just one day of conditioning and one day of plyometrics and agility drills each week or by doing less each of the days you work out.

Off-Season Conditioning Program

The conditioning program starts with six weeks of strides. Sprints start during week 7. The figure on page 51 illustrates strides and sprints. Court work starts in week 8. The more demanding final three weeks include a combination of strides, sprints, and court drills.

Percentage Estimation of Running Speed

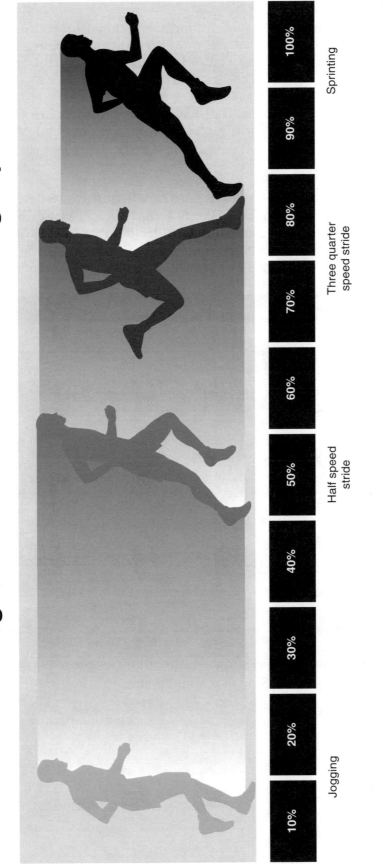

10%	20%	30%	40%	50%	60%	70%	80%	90%	100%

Jogging   Half speed stride   Three quarter speed stride   Sprinting

Strides

The strides start at 400 meters and work down to 100 meters. Strides are good-effort runs with smooth form. When running strides, athletes should go about three-quarter speed, somewhere between a sprint and half speed.

Sprints

Sprints are all-out efforts. The distances for sprints are 60 yards and less. For information about sprinting technique, refer to chapter 7 on speed training.

Court Drills

On-court drills and stair running are excellent ways to develop the anaerobic energy systems needed for basketball and should be performed with all-out efforts. They're also a good transition from running on the track to basketball-specific movements on the court in preparation for the first practice. Use the following drills after seven weeks of strides and sprints on the track.

FIVE-AND-A-HALFS

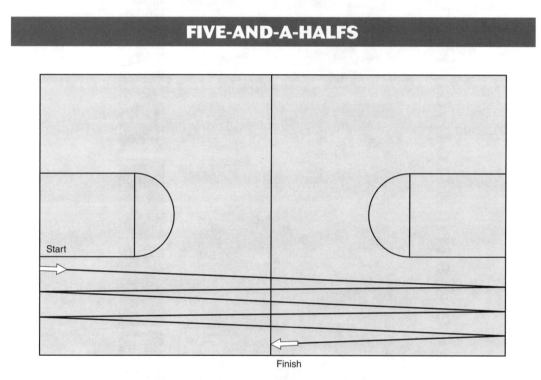

Start at one baseline and sprint to the other baseline. Repeat this five times and finish at halfcourt. Stay in a straight line.

HALFCOURT, FULLCOURT

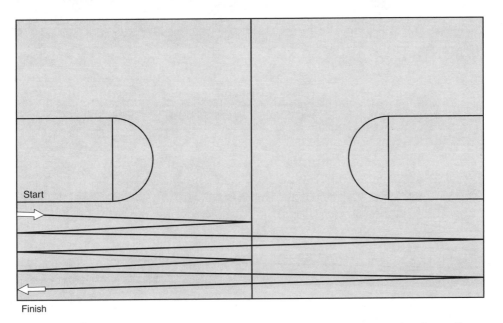

Start at one baseline, sprint to halfcourt, and sprint back to the baseline. Then sprint to the other baseline, sprint back, and sprint to halfcourt. Sprint back again, sprint to the other baseline, and sprint back. Stay in a straight line.

60-SECOND SIDELINE DRILL

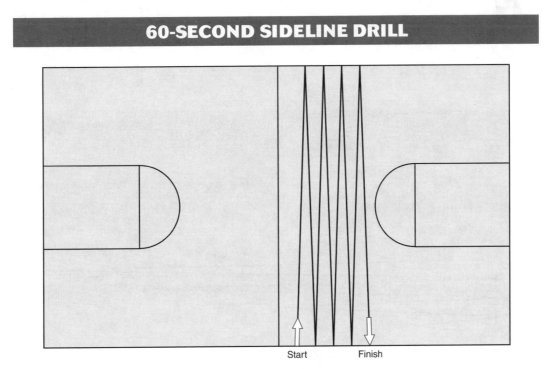

Start at one sideline and sprint to the other sideline and back. Repeat as many times as possible in 60 seconds. Over and back is 2 repetitions. Try to achieve 17 or more repetitions. Stay in a straight line.

SUICIDES

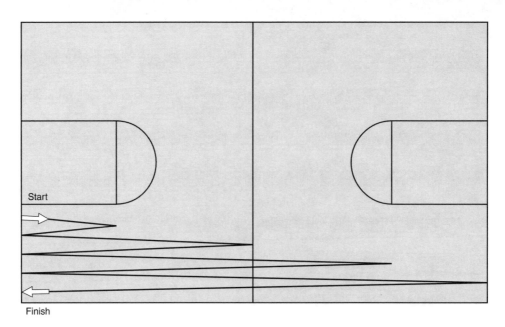

Start at the baseline, sprint to the free-throw line, and sprint back to the baseline. Then sprint to halfcourt, sprint back to the baseline, sprint to the far free-throw line and back. Finally sprint to the other baseline and back. Stay in a straight line.

REVERSE SUICIDES

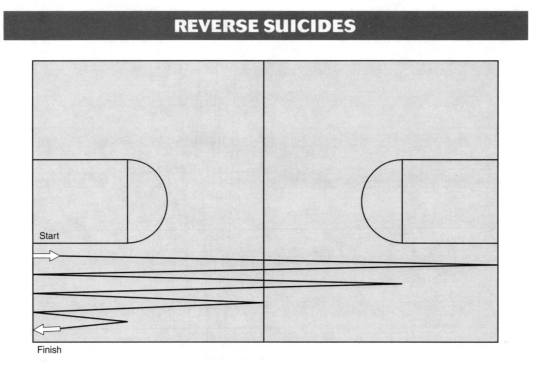

These are like suicides, but go from long to short. Start at the baseline and sprint to the other baseline and back. Then sprint to the far free-throw line and back. Sprint to halfcourt and back. Then sprint to the closer free-throw line and back to the baseline.

TWELVE-WEEK OFF-SEASON CONDITIONING PROGRAM

Each off-season conditioning session is mapped out for you in table 3-1. Note the type of drills, distances, number of repetitions, and the rest intervals for each workout.

For example, on day 2 of week 2, after warming up and stretching out, you stride a 400, then rest three minutes; stride another 400, then rest three minutes; repeat four times. After your last 400 you rest for three minutes and then start the 200s. A one-and-a-half minute rest is allowed between each of the four 200 strides you'll perform. Then, cool down and stretch. After the workout, record your best 400 time and your best 200 time to monitor your progress.

Table 3-1
12-Week Off-Season Basketball-Specific Conditioning Program

Week	Day	Drill	Distance	Rest interval	Best time
1	1	Stride	4 × 400	3 minutes	——————
	2	Stride	4 × 400	3 minutes	——————
2	1	Stride	6 × 400	3 minutes	——————
	2	Stride	4 × 400	3 minutes	——————
		Stride	4 × 200	1.5 minutes	——————
3	1	Stride	4 × 400	3 minutes	——————
		Stride	4 × 200	1.5 minutes	——————
	2	Stride	4 × 400	3 minutes	——————
		Stride	6 × 200	1.5 minutes	——————
4	1	Stride	12 × 200	1.5 minutes	——————
	2	Stride	12 × 200	1.5 minutes	——————
5	1	Stride	8 × 200	1.5 minutes	——————
		Stride	8 × 100	45 seconds	——————
	2	Stride	8 × 200	1.5 minutes	——————
		Stride	8 × 100	45 seconds	——————
6	1	Stride	8 × 200	1 minute	——————
		Stride	8 × 100	30 seconds	——————
	2	Stride	8 × 200	1 minute	——————
		Stride	8 × 100	30 seconds	——————
7	1	Stride	2 × 100	30 seconds	——————
		Stride	2 × 80	30 seconds	——————
		Sprint*	12 × 60	30 seconds	——————
	2	Stride	2 × 100	30 seconds	——————
		Stride	2 × 80	30 seconds	——————
		Sprint	12 × 40	30 seconds	——————

* Do not time yourself when sprinting, have a coach or friend time you.

(continued)

Table 3-1
(continued)

Week	Day	Drill	Distance	Rest interval	Best time
8	1	Stride	2 × 100	30 seconds	_____
		Stride	2 × 80	30 seconds	_____
		Sprint	12 × 60	30 seconds	_____
	2	COURT WORK			
		5 1/2s × 2-3 times		1.5 minutes	_____
		Halfcourt, full court × 2-3 times		1.5 minutes	_____
		60-second side-line drill × 1**		(Do last)	_____
9	1	Stride	2 × 100	30 seconds	_____
		Stride	2 × 80	30 seconds	_____
		Sprint	12 × 40	25 seconds	_____
	2	COURT WORK			
		5 1/2s × 2-3 times		1.5 minutes	_____
		Halfcourt, full court × 2-3 times		1.5 minutes	_____
		60-second side-line drill × 2 times		3 minutes	_____
		Do in a circuit			
10	1	Stride	2 × 100	30 seconds	_____
		Stride	2 × 80	30 seconds	_____
		Sprint	2 × 60	25 seconds	_____
		Sprint	2 × 40	25 seconds	_____
		Sprint	2 × 20	25 seconds	_____
		Sprint	4 × 10	25 seconds	_____
		Sprint	2 × 20	25 seconds	_____
		Sprint	2 × 40	25 seconds	_____
		Sprint	2 × 60	25 seconds	_____
	2	COURT WORK			
		5 1/2s × 2-4 times		1.5 minutes	_____
		Halfcourt, full court × 2-4 times		1.5 minutes	_____
		60-second side-line drill × 2 times		3 minutes	_____
11	1	5 1/2s × 1		1 minute	_____
		Halfcourt, full court × 1		1 minute	_____
		Suicides × 2-3 times		1 minute	_____
		Reverse suicides × 2-3 times		1 minute	_____
		60-second side-line drill × 2 times		2 minutes	_____
	2	5 1/2s × 2-4 times		1 minute	_____
		Halfcourt, full court × 2 times		1 minute	_____
		Suicides × 2-4 times		1 minute	_____
		Reverse suicides × 2-4 times		1 minute	_____
		60-second side-line drill × 2 times		2 minutes	_____
12	1	5 1/2s × 2 times		1 minute	_____
		Halfcourt, full court × 2 times		1 minute	_____
		Suicides × 2-4 times		1 minute	_____
		Reverse suicides × 2-4 times		1 minute	_____
		60-second side-line drill × 2 times		2 minutes	_____
	2	5 1/2s × 2 times		1 minute	_____
		Halfcourt, full court × 2 times		1 minute	_____
		Suicides × 2-4 times		1 minute	_____
		Reverse suicides × 2-4 times		1 minute	_____
		60-second side-line drill × 2 times		2 minutes	_____

** For 60-second side-line drill record repetitions, not time.

Gary Payton works on his conditioning program with strength and conditioning coach Bob Medina.

STAIRS

For variety in your court work conditioning program you may run stairs if they are available. Repetitions will depend on the total number of stairs. Suggested repetitions: 10 to 20.

Conditioning for Other Seasons

The 12-week off-season conditioning program provides an excellent base for starting preseason practice. From there you'll need to take your conditioning to another level and make it more basketball-specific.

Preseason Conditioning

Preseason is the time between the first official practice in the fall up to the first game. This is the time a coach tries to fine-tune players' off-season conditioning into quality basketball conditioning. If you followed the off-season program, you'll go into preseason in very good shape. That way you can concentrate on basketball and not struggle with your conditioning.

In-Season Conditioning

During basketball season, a conditioning program consists of quality practices and intense games. If your practice consists of intense all-out drills, running the court hard, and high-effort defensive work, you don't need extra conditioning.

If not, you can add the on-court conditioning drills from the off-season conditioning program to stay at a high level. Also, consider using these drills if you're not getting much playing time.

Postseason Conditioning

Most schools' basketball teams end their seasons in March. The postseason is the time from your last game to the start of your off-season conditioning program.

The postseason is the "active rest" time of the year. Initially, you will want to recover physically from a long basketball season. But during postseason you should stay fit by playing other sports or by working out in the beginning phase of the weight-training program.

If you're not getting much running from other sports or pickup basketball games, you need to do some general fitness activities such as biking, jogging, swimming, or hiking. Workouts for 20 to 40 minutes on conditioning machines such as stair climbers, rowers, and stationary bikes are another option. Jogging two miles a few times a week is another activity some athletes prefer.

In chapter 10 we provide the 12-week power conditioning program. This total program shows where your conditioning workouts fit into your training schedule.

PART

II

Power
Base Strength

STRENGTH TRAINING

ost players want to become stronger and more powerful. They know it's only a myth that strength training hurts the shooting touch. They've seen how Alonzo Mourning, Anthony Mason, and other muscular NBA stars have used their strength to great advantage, and they want to do the same.

The problem is that many athletes don't know how to strength train properly. So they either avoid strengthening exercises and lifting or they train incorrectly and injure themselves. In this chapter we'll show how to add muscle the smart way, with correct technique for resistance exercises and lifts.

Dan Majerle of the Miami Heat has seen the positive effects of strength and weight training, "Strength training has given me the strength to make it through the long and grinding NBA seasons averaging over 40 minutes a game throughout my career."

A well-designed, functional strength-training program for basketball improves performance, reduces the risk of injury, and keeps players motivated. Increases in strength, speed, quickness, power, and flexibility enhance performance. Injuries are less common because muscles and connective tissue are stronger, and joints have increased range of motion. Motivation stays high because athletes' confidence grows with greater physical capability and more frequent on-court success.

"Strength training," says Kevin Johnson of the Phoenix Suns, "has helped give me the power and durability to consistently penetrate and challenge the NBA's best big men night after night, year after year." And Anfernee "Penny" Hardaway of the Orlando Magic adds his support of strength training, "Strength training has helped me mentally and physically. Knowing I've increased my strength not only increases my confidence but also helps my defensive and offensive performance."

This chapter presents solid information for developing a total strength-training program for basketball. We begin in the center of the body with

© NBA Photos/Richard Lewis

Tim Hardaway shows his range while taking a long 3-point shot.

the most highly recommended abdominal exercises. Then we present a series of strength-training exercises covering the entire body.

We will clearly explain and illustrate the exercises. But if you aren't exactly sure about the proper technique, consult your conditioning coach. Then start putting more muscle into your game!

ABDOMINAL EXERCISES

Let's start with the abdominals. Ab strength is essential to the athlete because it helps protect the body from injury, notably to the lower-back area. It also helps create greater stability throughout the midsection and aids the spinal erectors in postural alignments of the vertebral column and pelvis. Greater abdominal and hip flexor strength may also help increase running speed, stamina, and knee lift.

CONDITIONING TIP

Don't pull on neck with hands, let abdominals do the work. Breathe normally and don't hold your breath.

We have evaluated many abdominal exercises and have selected 12 exercises that offer a wide variety of functional movements. Use these exercises to develop both abdominal strength and endurance, just like the pros.

Prayer crunches demonstrated by Juwan Howard.

ABDOMINAL EXERCISE DICTIONARY

The following definitions of key terms will help you understand the abdominal exercises in this chapter.

hip flexors—The hip flexors raise the legs toward the chest when the upper body is fixed and move the chest toward the legs when the legs are fixed.

flexors of the spine—The rectus abdominus and internal/external obliques flex or curl the spine.

rotators of the spine—The rectus abdominus, internal/external obliques, semispinalis, multifidus, rotatores, and levatores muscles contribute to the rotation of the spine.

prime mover—Primary muscle or muscles involved in a movement.

assistor—Aids the prime movers with a movement.

stabilizer—Usually a muscle in a nonmoving, isometric contraction stabilizing one body part so another body part, usually involving a prime mover, has something to pull against.

BENT-LEG RAISES

1. Take a slightly wider than shoulder-width grip on a chin-up bar and keep your upper torso relaxed.
2. Raise your knees all the way to your chest each time. The more you curl your spine at the top of the movement, the greater your abdominal involvement.

Prime mover: hip flexors
Stabilizers: abdominals and obliques

STRAIGHT-LEG RAISES

1. Take a slightly wider than shoulder-width grip on a chin-up bar and keep your upper torso relaxed.

2. Raise your legs until your feet touch the bar. Your pelvis should rock forward as you raise your legs. This guarantees maximum abdominal involvement.

3. Hold for a second or so, then lower legs back to the starting position.

Note: It's important that you lower your legs slowly enough so you don't start swinging; bend your knees slightly throughout the exercise.

Prime mover: hip flexors

Stabilizers: abdominals and obliques

PRAYER CRUNCHES (FEET DOWN)

1. Lie in the standard bent-leg sit-up position with your lower back flat against the floor.

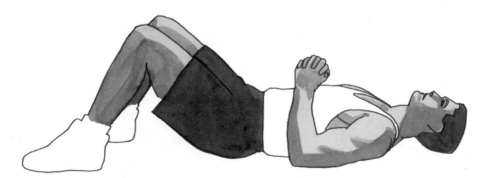

2. Raise your shoulders and upper back about 30 to 45 degrees off the ground.
3. Hold for a second or so, then slowly return to starting position. Keep your arms in place but relaxed throughout the exercise.

Prime movers: abdominals and obliques
Stabilizer: hip flexors

ROTARY CRUNCHES (FEET UP)

1. Start in bent-knee sit-up position, both legs off the floor so both your hips and your knees form right angles.
2. Place both hands behind your head.
3. Raise shoulders 12 to 18 inches off the ground, turn your right elbow toward left knee, return to the ground. Then raise up and rotate left elbow to right knee. (This counts as one repetition; perform these repetitions rapidly.)

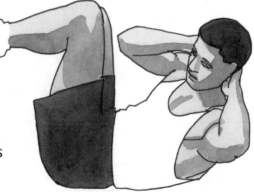

Prime movers: rectus abdominis, internal/external obliques, semispinalis, multifidus, rotatores, and levatores muscles
Stabilizer: hip flexors

STRAIGHT-LEG CRUNCHES

1. Lie on your back with your lower back flat against the ground in the flexed position, legs straight out, and hands on your thighs, palms down.

2. Flex your abdominals as you lift your shoulders slightly off the ground and slide your hands down your thighs.

3. Hold for a count, then return.

Prime movers: abdominals and obliques

Stabilizer: hip flexors

ROTARY CRUNCHES (FEET DOWN)

1. Lie in bent-knee sit-up position and slowly raise your shoulders and upper back off the ground. Your right elbow should turn toward (but not touch) your left knee.

2. Hold at peak for at least one second, then slowly return to starting position. Repeat with the left elbow turning toward the right knee.

Prime movers: rectus abdominis, internal/external obliques, semispinalis, multifidus, rotatores, and levatores muscles

Stabilizer: hip flexors

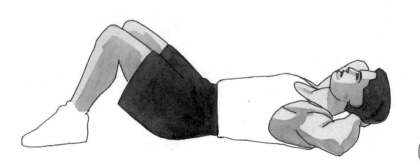

CRUNCHES (FEET UP)

1. Start in bent-knee position with legs off the floor.

2. Quickly raise upper back and shoulders off the floor, then lower and repeat. Perform these quickly, being careful not to pull against the neck or flap the elbows; use the abdominals.

Prime movers: abdominals and obliques

Stabilizer: hip flexors

QUICK TOUCHES (STRAIGHT LEGS)

1. Lie on the floor with your back down and legs straight up.

2. Keeping legs straight, reach up and touch toes quickly. Don't completely return your back flat to the floor between repetitions.

Prime movers: abdominals and obliques

Stabilizer: hip flexors (in isometric contraction)

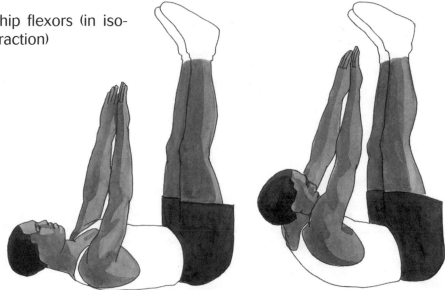

KNEE ROCK BACKS

1. Begin in bent-knee sit-up position, feet on the floor, with arms extended a few inches from your sides, palms down.

2. Rock back until your knees hit your chest and your lower back comes off the floor. Curl your spine at the top of the movement to exercise your abdominals more.

3. Lower and repeat.

Prime mover: hip flexors
Stabilizers: abdominals and obliques

LYING SIX-INCH LEG RAISES

1. Lie on your back. Place hands, palms down, under pelvis. Your hands and arms should function as a cradle to prevent your back from arching.

2. Keep your head and shoulders up with abdominals flexed to flatten your lower back against the floor. This limits the strain on the lower back.

3. Raise the legs about 18 inches off the floor; then lower to about 12 inches. Repeat up to 18 inches, then down to 12 inches.

4. You may also alternately flutter kick or criss cross legs out and in over one another.

Note: If you feel pain in your lower back, your abdominals may not yet be strong enough to do this exercise. Skip it until you sufficiently strengthen your abdominals.

Prime mover: hip flexors; criss crosses include thigh abductors and adductors
Stabilizers: abdominals and obliques

STRAIGHT-UPS

1. Lie flat on your back with your arms at your sides for support. The legs should be together and vertical.

2. Raise legs and hips approximately six to eight inches straight up. Return to ground briefly, then repeat.

Prime movers: abdominals and obliques
Stabilizer: hip flexors

SIDE-UPS

1. Lie on your left side, left hand on right obliques and right hand on side of head. The legs are straight down and in line with torso, with the top leg resting over and in front of bottom leg.

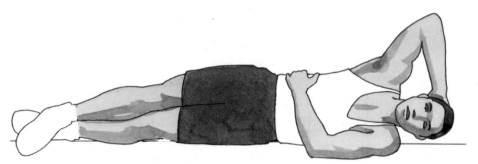

2. Raise left shoulder six to eight inches upwards off ground, squeezing your right obliques and abdominals. Your right shoulder will move toward your right hip.

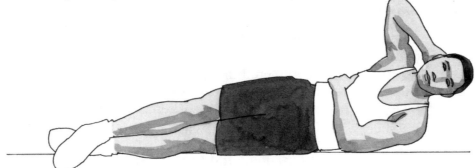

3. Return to ground and repeat.
4. Switch sides and repeat exercise.

Prime movers: rectus abdominis, obliques, and inter-transversari
Stabilizers: hip flexors, gluteals, and muscles of the thigh

BASICS OF STRENGTH TRAINING

Now let's move to the weight room. But before you start pumping iron, let's review some essential information and safety considerations for strength-training exercises. Even if you're an experienced lifter, we encourage you to review this section. Better to do a little lifting precisely than a lot of lifting incorrectly.

Determining Loads

Before performing any type of lift, you should first adjust the equipment and weight to fit your individual needs. For optimal results you have to know how much weight you should be lifting. To determine weight loads for each lift, you can use (a) the trial-and-error method, (b) a percentage of body weight, or (c) a more scientific approach based on percentages of your strength.

Methods (b) and (c) require some calculation, which you can find in most instructional manuals on weightlifting. To keep things simple, we've decided to present the trial-and-error procedure. Here's how it works.

1. Warm up with a light weight to prevent injury to the muscle or muscles that will be performing the lift.
2. For the first set of the exercises, choose a comfortable weight that you can lift without straining while completing prescribed repetitions.
3. Gradually increase the weight over time to become stronger and better conditioned.

When using the trial-and-error method, establish a true training resistance load for each lift. Choose a light, comfortable weight to begin, then add weight until you can feel the amount of resistance needed to perform the exercise correctly for a desired number of repetitions.

Sets and Reps

Sets and repetitions are closely related to loads. Sets refer to each time an exercise is performed for a given number of repetitions. Reps, or repetitions, refer to the number of fully completed movements of the exercise performed during a set. Usually, the heavier the loads, the lower the number of reps. The lighter the loads, the higher the number of reps.

If you're younger than high school age, please refer to "prepubescent weight training" in the Glossary. Young athletes should lift lighter weights with higher repetitions (12 to 15) per set for safety and health reasons.

Breathing

When you walk through a weight room, the easy way to spot the rookies is to check who is holding their breaths. The rookies are the ones with the puffed-out cheeks, looking as if they're ready to burst. That's bad technique and bad for you. Always breathe when you're lifting.

Breathe out (exhale) during the most difficult phase of the exercise, for example, when raising the bar during an arm curl. Breathe in (inhale) during the easiest phase of the exercise, for example, when lowering the bar during the arm curl.

It's probably a good idea to inhale before starting the movement, to hold your breath during the beginning of the movement, and to exhale when you've completed two-thirds of the exercise. This method of breathing will allow for a large blood return to the heart and thus reduce heart distress.

If an individual holds his or her breath throughout the exercise, cardiac problems such as elevated blood pressure and irregular heartbeats may occur. An athlete who fails to breathe properly when exerting effort, especially during weight training, may experience a *Valsalva effect*. This reaction includes a rise in blood pressure, during which dizziness or fainting may occur.

One exception to the breathing rules for weightlifters involves the explosive, Olympic-type lifts. When performing the power clean, the exhalation of air comes after the squat-and-catch phase and before the ascent. During the ascent, the lifter may produce short inhalations followed by short exhalations.

Lifting Belt

A weightlifting belt provides added support to the muscles surrounding the lower spine. Using a belt aids particularly the abdominal muscles; it gives them something to push against when performing a high-effort, maximum or submaximum, multijoint exercise like a squat.

Most weight rooms and gyms have belts on site for this purpose. One caution: Just because you're wearing a belt doesn't mean you can be sloppy in your lifting technique and still avoid injury. A belt is no substitute for proper technique during the exercise.

Adequate Spacing

Give yourself plenty of room to perform each exercise free of other people, machines, equipment, etc. Make sure any weights (dumbbells, bars, or plates) are off the floor in and around the training area. The floor surface should be dry and smooth, free of any debris.

Far too many accidents happen because of sloppy weight-room maintenance by athletes. Be responsible for the facility and respectful toward others, and avoid careless mishaps.

Spotting

Spotting involves observing or physically assisting an athlete during an exercise. This assistance may include helping the athlete raise, balance, or lower the weight while performing an exercise. A spotter may have to provide a great deal of assistance, so the spotter should never spot for a lift of a weight greater than he or she can handle. Most often, the lifter requires only a little assistance during the end of a set when fatigue strikes.

When you're the spotter, be sure always to keep your eyes on the bar and the position of the lifter's body. Look for a breakdown in technique, a loss of balance, a sticking point (no movement) during the exercise, or a bar moving out of the proper exercise groove. When spotting dumbbell exercises, please grab the lifter's wrists or forearms so that you can help guide the dumbbells safely back into the proper lifting groove.

Whenever you perform a free-weight lift, check how the plates look on the barbell beforehand. Is the weight distributed equally on both sides? Are the collars in place and fastened tightly on both ends of the barbell?

Showing proper spotting techniques, strength and conditioning coach Bill Foran spots Alonzo Mourning while he does the dumbbell incline press.

Lift-Off and Return

Exercises such as the bench press and the seated shoulder press may require a lift-off to start the movement. The most common and correct lift-off technique is as follows:

1. The spotter or lifter counts to three.

2. On three, the spotter and the lifter, together, lift the weight to the starting position.

3. Once the lifter has the weight stable by himself or herself, the spotter removes his or her hands from the bar or weight.

4. The lifter then lowers the weight to begin the exercise.

Usually the spotter places his or her hands evenly along the bar, with one hand over the bar and the other hand underneath the bar. This allows for a well-balanced and well-controlled lift-off. The spotter helps the lifter both out of and back into the rack.

The lifter must control both the lowering and raising phases of the lift. Perform each repetition with a smooth, controlled movement. When performing explosive movements, however, complete each repetition quickly with proper technique.

Rest Intervals

Rest periods play a major role in establishing each muscle's potential strength or endurance level. The longer the rest period between each working set, the more time a muscle has to replenish its energy supply. Therefore, the muscle has a greater potential of becoming stronger.

Conversely, a shorter rest period (say 30 to 90 seconds) will allow for an increase in potential endurance while causing a decrease in potential strength. Consider these two factors when determining rest periods for resistance training.

Don't wait until your body has cooled down between sets before you begin to perform the next set. Such a delay increases the chance of injuries; your body has to handle heavy weight when it's no longer fully prepared. In most cases, three to five minutes is enough rest.

Exercise Sequence

In general, you should first exercise the large muscle groups, then exercise the small muscle groups. If you do a total-body program in the same day, split your body in half and follow this philosophy for both upper-body and lower-body exercises. Some people have target body parts or exercises that they want to do first, or prefatigue their muscles, before doing the rest of the program. In these special cases, you may do these exercises first.

STRENGTH-TRAINING EXERCISE TECHNIQUES AND ILLUSTRATIONS

This section contains illustrations and brief explanations of the correct and safe technique for each basketball-conditioning exercise. Very few athletes are capable of perfect technique on all exercises, because execution varies depending on individual differences, range of motion, grips, stances, and so on. Try to follow these directions. And, to be on the safe side, have a qualified coach or instructor evaluate your lifting technique, even if you've been using weights for some time.

SQUAT

1. Using a medium-to-wide overhand grip, raise the elbows up in the air to create a muscular shelf (the posterior deltoids and upper trapezius) on which the bar can ride. Do not place the bar on your neck; it should be below your neck.

2. Position both feet and hips under the bar as you straighten your legs to get the bar out of the rack.

3. Step back and get in a set position; stance should be slightly wider than hip-width with toes pointed slightly out. Your eyes, head, shoulders, and chest should all be up with a tight back throughout the lift.

4. Squat down slowly, leading with the hips, until the thighs are parallel to the ground. Do not bounce at the bottom. Make sure that the knees are in line with the toes and don't allow knees to stray inside or outside normal tracking. Keep the weight evenly displaced over the feet; do not shift weight forward to the toes or allow knees to be in front of the toes in the bottom parallel position.

5. Raise the bar slowly by straightening out the hips and knees while maintaining correct body position. Keep the hips underneath you; don't round your back and lean forward on your feet.

6. When you complete the set, slowly walk the bar back into the rack with both feet and hips underneath the bar. Squat down and lower bar onto the rack.

Spotter: From behind, help partner out of rack. Squat each rep with partner with hands underneath bar or underneath arms near chest. Assist, only if necessary, by grabbing bar or chest from underneath and having both of you squat the weight up to a safe position. Walk forward and help your partner safely into the rack. Hold bar in and tell your partner to lower the bar. Adjust not only the bar rack, but the safety bars inside the rack to just below parallel to catch bar if needed.

HANG PULLS

1. Stand with feet hip-width apart and the bar near your shins (refer to power clean beginning position.).
2. Use a closed pronated wide grip.
3. Stand up slowly with bar. Keep the back and legs tight, and arms straight.
4. Cock bar and slide it down thighs to power-pulling position, just above the knees.
5. Initiate pull with the legs, hips, and back, while keeping arms straight.
6. Thrust shoulders backward and up, and the hips forward and up.
7. Straighten legs and extend up onto the toes.
8. Pull with the arms, keeping the bar close to the body.
9. As the bar reaches the upper chest, bend the knees to prevent back strain.
10. When lowering the bar, brush it off the thighs to protect lower back as knees bend upon impact.
11. Return to step 4 to do more reps, to step 3 to return bar to the ground.

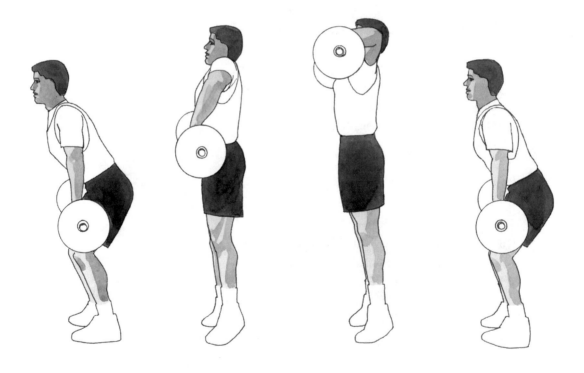

HANG CLEAN

1. Follow the hang pull technique progression to step 9, except use shoulder-width grip for racking.
2. Prepare for the catch or rack of the bar by lowering the body to a one-eighth to one-quarter squat position, then let the bar descend.
3. Rotate wrists backward around the bar with elbows high and out in front of bar. Carry the bar on shoulders with a bending or cushioning of the legs.
4. Stand up and rack bar. For more reps, use steps 10 and 11 of the hang pulls.

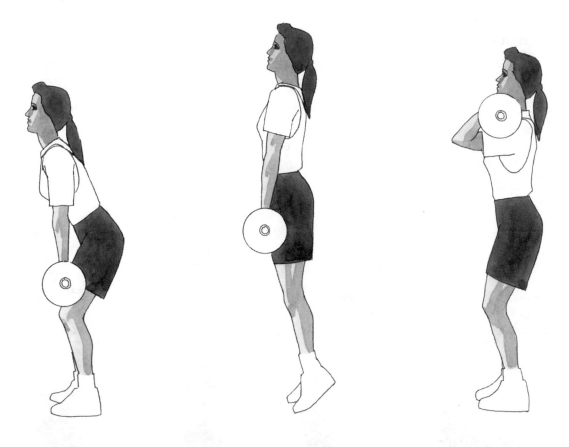

CONDITIONING TIP

A) Coach from the side.
B) Use jumping analogy with the shoulders over the bar for the start of the second pulling phase of the lift, jump first, then pull bar up.
C) Drag thumbs along your rib cage with high elbows and no looping or reverse curling of the bar. This helps keep the bar close to the body during the second pull.

POWER CLEAN AND CLEAN PULL FROM THE GROUND

Starting position:

1. Stand with feet hip-width, bar touching shins.
2. Keep back flat and tight with shoulders over the bar.
3. Grip the bar with a closed pronated grip (palms facing body).

First pull:

4. Pull bar from the floor slowly and smoothly, using the legs. Shoulders remain over the bar and back stays flat.
5. Keep the bar close to the body and the hips down until bar clears the knees.
6. Raise your hips slightly to prepare for the scoop or second pulling phase of the lift. Refer to step 5 of hang pulls.
7. Follow progression of desired lift. Always bend knees slightly to protect lower back after the second pull and rack.

Note: When racking, don't catch too deep or wide with stance; keep grip shoulder-width to protect elbows.

LEG PRESS OR HIP SLED

1. Lie with back flat on machine and buttocks touching pad. Use handles to pull buttocks up against pad and hold this position (especially when legs are at the bottom of the lift).

2. Release safety catches and turn them out while raising the weight until the legs are almost, but not completely, locked out.

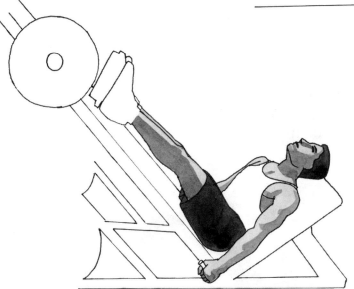

3. Lower the weight until the legs and thighs have a 75- to 90-degree angle between them.

4. At the bottom of the lift, the knees should not be in front of the toes. If they are, place the feet higher on the foot platform or pedals, if possible. Make sure your buttocks are on the pad, not off it with spine rolled up. Always keep the back flat .

5. Slowly bring the weight back up almost, but not quite, to full extension.

6. Turn in safety locks and slowly lower the weight.

LYING HAMSTRING CURLS (DOUBLE OR SINGLE LEG)

1. Lie face down on the machine with pads behind the heels.
2. Hold on to handles, if available.

3. Curl the legs up; keep flat on the bench until pads touch, or almost touch, buttocks or back of thigh.

4. Return slowly to the starting position.

Note: You may also do single-leg lying hamstring curls.

STEP-UPS
(WITH BARBELL, DUMBBELL, OR BODY WEIGHT ONLY)

1. Start with the barbell on the shoulders. You may use dumbbells held at your sides.
2. Step up with the right leg onto the bench or platform and bring the trailing left leg up to a standing position. The bench or platform height should bring your thigh parallel to the floor when stepping up.
3. Step down under control with the right leg first, then the left leg, to standing position.
4. Repeat this sequence, leading with the opposite leg; alternate legs through set.

FRONT LUNGE
(WITH DUMBBELL, BARBELL, OR BODY WEIGHT ONLY)

1. Start in a standing position with dumbbells at your sides. You can also use your body weight only or a barbell on your shoulders.
2. Step forward, keeping the head, shoulders, and torso vertical.
3. Make sure the shoulders and hips remain square. Maintain your balance as you lunge forward until your thigh is parallel to the floor.
4. Keep the trail leg as straight as you can without touching the knee to the ground.
5. Push off and step back to the starting position.
6. Repeat with the opposite leg, alternating until you complete the set.

SIDE LUNGE
(WITH BARBELL, DUMBBELL, OR BODY WEIGHT ONLY)

1. Start in standing position with dumbbells at your sides or in front of you. You can also use your body weight only or a barbell on your shoulders.
2. Step to the side, keeping the head, shoulders, and torso upright until the thigh is almost parallel to the floor and the trailing leg is slightly bent.
3. Push off and step back to the starting position.
4. Repeat with the opposite leg, alternating until you complete the set.

LEG EXTENSIONS

1. Sit on the machine with pads on shins. Position the knees at the edge of the seat pad with room to move. Legs should be at least vertical and maybe a little farther back under the seat (but not too far under because that will put extra pressure on the knee joint). Use the handles if needed.

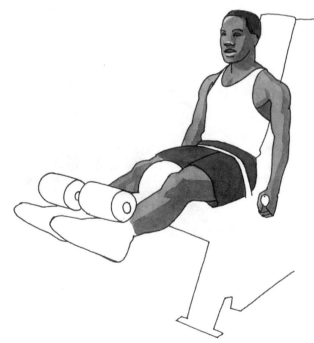

2. Slowly raise the legs up to fully extended position.

3. Lower the legs back down, under control.

STANDING SINGLE-LEG HAMSTRING CURL

1. Start with the roll pad just above the heel and thigh on support pad.

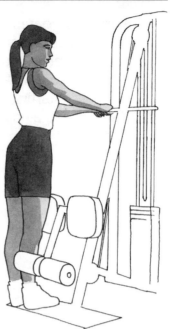

2. Raise the leg upward, keeping the thigh on support pad, and heel moving toward or touching the buttocks at the top, if possible.

3. Lower under control to the straight-leg starting position while keeping the thigh on the support pad.

4. Make sure you do both legs, alternating or one leg at a time for reps or sets.

ADDUCTION MACHINE

1. Start in a seated position with the legs spread and the pads just above your knees. Hold on to the handles. Adjust the starting position; start as wide as possible.

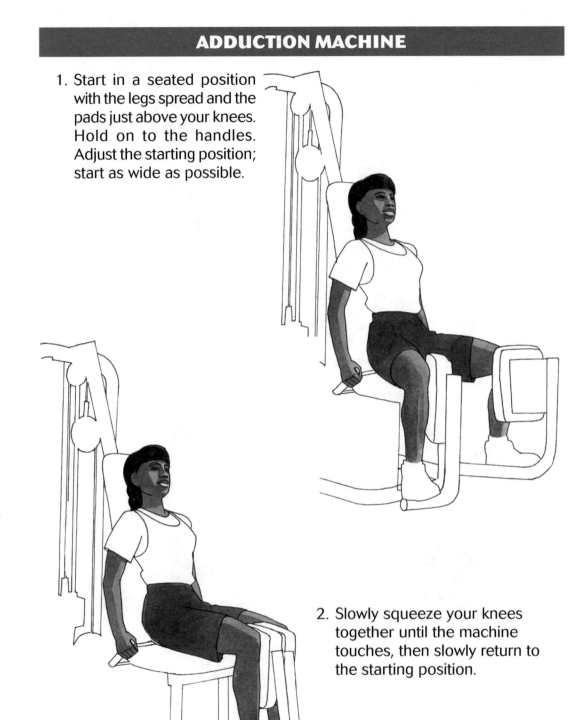

2. Slowly squeeze your knees together until the machine touches, then slowly return to the starting position.

Note: Exercise can be performed with single-leg low pulley, cables, tubing, and so forth.

ABDUCTION MACHINE

1. Start with the thighs together, seated with pads just above the knees. Hold on to the handles.

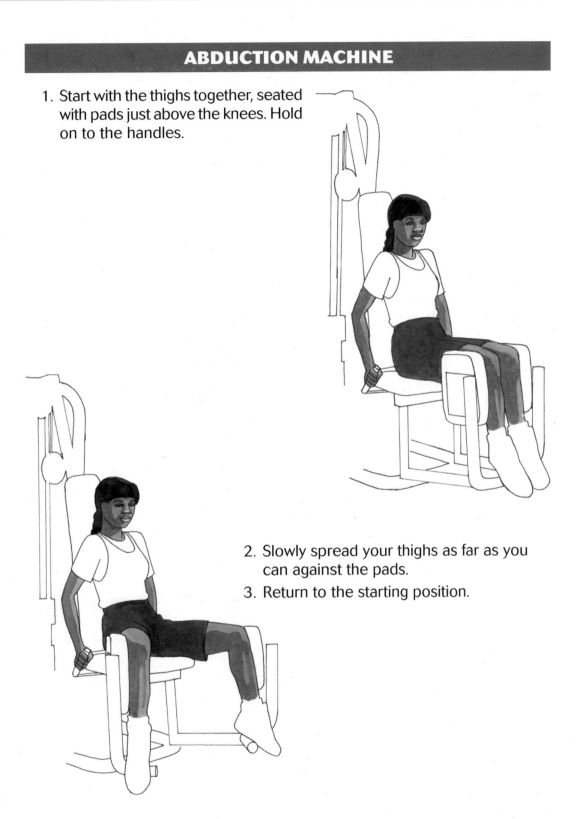

2. Slowly spread your thighs as far as you can against the pads.

3. Return to the starting position.

Note: Exercise can be performed with single-leg low pulley, cables, tubing, and so forth.

STANDING HEEL OR CALF RAISES

1. Stand on a platform with the pads on your shoulders, body straight, calves stretched, and heels down. For resistance, you may use a weight stack or your body weight. Use one or both feet.

2. Raise up onto your toes as high as you can and hold for a count. The only joint movement comes from ankle joint.

3. Return to the starting position for a count.

BACK EXTENSIONS

1. Place heels under heel pad and thighs on thigh pad with enough room to bend over.
2. Start at bottom with torso in a vertical position and hands behind head.

3. Raise torso until it is parallel to the ground or slightly above the thigh pad.

4. Control both raising and lowering phases and don't hyperextend your lower back at the top.

STRAIGHT-LEG DEAD LIFTS
(WITH BARBELL OR DUMBBELL)

1. Start in a standing position with a hip-width stance, holding the bar with straight arms in front of you.

2. With the knees straight or slightly bent, slowly bend over with straight back, lowering the bar along your legs to the top of your feet. Don't round the back.

3. Return slowly to starting position with a straight back to a full standing position. Don't bang weight on the floor or bounce at the bottom.

BARBELL BENCH PRESS

1. Lie flat on a bench with your head, shoulders, and buttocks touching the surface. Plant feet flat on the floor. Maintain this position throughout the lift.

2. Grips may vary, but in general grip the bar with hands slightly more than shoulder-width apart.

3. Your head should be not quite underneath the bar, so you may need help out of and back into the rack. This is so the bar won't hit the rack during the exercise.

4. From the starting position, slowly lower the bar to the nipple (four- to six-inch range) on your chest. Grooves vary; but this four- to six-inch range should fit everyone. Gently touch bar without bouncing and push up to full extension. Use spotter to rerack, if necessary.

Spotter: Use an alternating grip and on the count of three help the lifter to the starting-exercise position, then release the bar. Shadow the bar with the hands while not touching the bar unless needed (inside the lifter's grip). Assist with reracking the bar and let the lifter know when the bar is in the rack.

DUMBBELL BENCH PRESS

1. Once dumbbells are out of the rack, stand in front of the bench and sit on bench, placing dumbbells on your thighs. You may use your thighs to help kick up dumbbell to the starting position.

2. Lie flat on a bench with head, shoulders, and buttocks touching surface and feet flat on the floor. Place arms down, with dumbbells touching anterior deltoids in a barbell position.

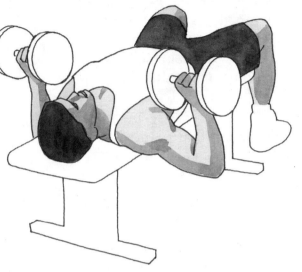

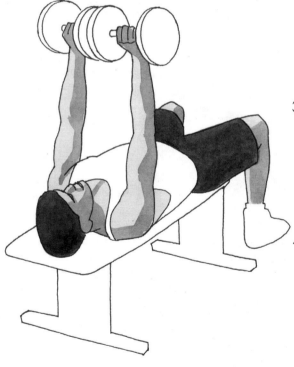

3. Slowly press both dumbbells to fully extended position over chest and gently touch them together between repetitions. Try to press each arm at the same speed and groove as the other arm.

4. Finish by lowering the dumbbells from over the chest to your thighs as you rock up off the bench. Don't drop dumbbells at the bottom or to the sides; this could cause an injury or damage the equipment.

Spotter: Spot dumbbells from behind by grabbing the wrists and guiding, if needed. Dumbbells may float inside, outside, below, or above desired exercise groove.

INCLINE BARBELL BENCH PRESS

1. Lie on the bench with the head, shoulders, and buttocks flat, and the feet flat on the floor. Maintain this position throughout the lift.

2. Use a medium-to-wide grip because of different technique grooves on the incline and flat bench.

3. From the overhead starting position, slowly lower the bar to your upper chest just below your clavicles and gently touch without bouncing. Push up to full extension. Exercise groove is different and higher on chest and to extended position.

Spotter: Same as on the bench press.

DUMBBELL INCLINE BENCH PRESS

1. Sit on the bench with dumbbells on your thighs.
2. Kick one knee and dumbbell at a time up to your chest to the starting position, touching your anterior deltoids with arms down.
3. Head, shoulders, and buttocks should be flat on bench, and feet should be firmly on the floor throughout exercise.

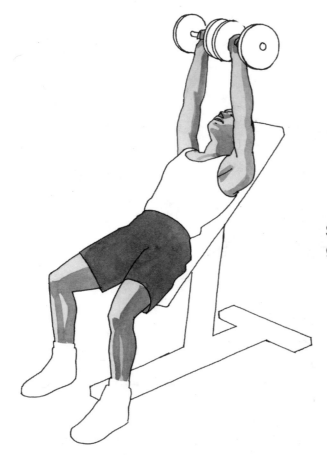

4. Slowly press both dumbbells to fully extended position, gently touching them at the top over your head. Return to starting position when set is complete and place dumbbells on your thighs before getting up off bench.

Spotter: Grab wrists and guide, if needed, from behind.

STANDING MILITARY PRESS

1. Follow power clean progression to get to starting point. Use shoulder-width grip with elbows under bar. Spotter should take a position behind lifter.

2. Slowly press bar to full extension over head (without arching back).

3. Lower bar to shoulders under control.

SEATED DUMBBELL SHOULDER PRESS

1. Sit on the end of the bench with back straight and feet balanced firmly on the floor.

2. Either curl up or kick up dumbbells one thigh at a time to starting position just over your outside shoulder.

3. Slowly press both dumbbells overhead and gently touch before lowering to starting position.

Spotter: Grab wrists and guide from behind (if necessary).

TRICEPS PRESS-DOWNS

1. Grip with palms down approximately 6 to 10 inches apart.
2. Keep arms and elbows fixed and in at your side.
3. Hands and bar start up around armpits.
4. Press down smoothly, moving only your forearms to full extension.
5. Return under control to starting position.

LYING TRICEPS EXTENSION

1. Lie flat on bench with head, shoulders, and buttocks touching surface and feet firmly on the floor. Maintain this position throughout lift.
2. Use a narrow grip and start with bar extended.

3. Slowly lower bar, keeping elbows in to the forehead
4. Extend bar to full lockout over shoulders. Forearms only should move; arms should be in a fixed (vertical, straight up and down) position.

BAR DIPS

1. Start in straight-arm, locked-out position with body erect.
2. Slowly lower body under control with elbows in and pointing behind you until shoulders go below elbows. A 90-degree angle between arm and forearm is minimum depth.
3. Press back up to fully extended straight arms.

PUSH-UPS

1. Place hands slightly wider than shoulders; keep legs and back straight while resting up on your toes.

2. Keep your body rigid in a straight line; push your body up to full extension.

3. Lower to within one inch of the floor.
4. Repeat for desired reps.

PULL-UPS: WIDE GRIP BEHIND THE HEAD

1. Hang from the bar with pronated grip and hands wider than shoulders, with body and arms straight.

2. Pull up until back of neck touches the bar, keeping legs fairly straight and without jerking the body.

3. Return slowly to starting hanging position with straight arms.

PULL-UPS: MEDIUM GRIP IN FRONT

1. Hang from bar with pronated grip and hands slightly wider than shoulder-width and body and arms hanging straight.
2. Pull up until chin is over bar, keeping legs fairly straight and without jerking the body.
3. Return slowly to starting position with arms straight.

WIDE-GRIP LAT PULL-DOWNS BEHIND HEAD

1. Sit on a bench; put legs underneath the thigh pads (if available) with the torso vertical. Make sure the arms are straight at the top starting position with hands in a wide pronated position.

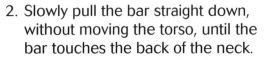

2. Slowly pull the bar straight down, without moving the torso, until the bar touches the back of the neck.

3. Return under control to the straight-arm starting position.

NARROW-GRIP LAT PULL-DOWNS IN FRONT

1. Sit on a bench. Put the legs underneath thigh pads (if available) with the torso vertical. Make sure the arms are straight at the top starting position with a shoulder-width pronated grip.

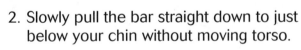

2. Slowly pull the bar straight down to just below your chin without moving torso.

3. Under control, return the bar to the starting position.

LOW-PULLEY SEATED LAT ROW

1. Seated on a pad with the legs slightly bent, place the feet on the bar or pedals; with the torso in a forward-leaning position, grab the handles with straight arms.

2. Slowly pull back on the handles with the arms and hands to stomach or low-chest position, while the lower back and torso move from a forward lean to a slightly backward lean during the pulling phase. Keep the knees bent.

3. Slowly return to the starting position.

DUMBBELL LAT ROW

1. Place left hand and left knee on the bench with torso parallel to the ground.

2. Right arm is straight or hanging with dumbbell; right leg is slightly bent on toes for balance.

3. Pull dumbbell up to outside shoulder area with a high elbow at the top of pull. Touch the shoulder. Don't jerk the weight up; use a steady pull.

4. Slowly lower the weight back to starting position.

5. Switch arms after set is completed.

LATERAL SHOULDER FLY MACHINE

1. Sit with your back against the pad, feet on the floor, and pads on forearms.

2. Slowly raise the forearms and elbows to above shoulder joint.

3. Slowly return to the starting position.

DUMBBELL UPRIGHT ROW

1. Standing with arms straight, rest dumbbells against your thighs with thumbs in and facing each other.

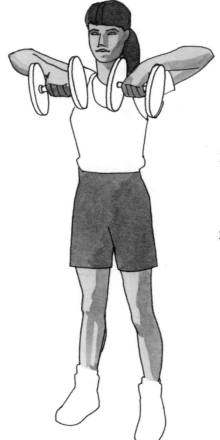

2. Pull dumbbells straight up the body, without swinging them out away from the body, to just below the chin with high elbows at the top. Bend knees slightly.

3. Slowly lower dumbbells under control through the same groove to the starting position.

BARBELL UPRIGHT ROW

1. Stand straight, with the bar resting against the thighs, arms straight, and hands six to eight inches apart in a pronated grip.

2. Pull the barbell straight up the body, without swinging it out away from the body, to just below the chin with high elbows at the top. Bend knees slightly.

3. Slowly lower the bar in the same groove to the starting position.

SEATED DUMBBELL LATERAL SHOULDER RAISES

1. Sit on the end of a bench with torso vertical and arms with dumbbells hanging down straight at your sides. Keep feet firmly on the floor.

2. Slowly raise dumbbells, with knuckles up and elbows slightly bent, to slightly above the shoulders. Pause at the top.

3. Lower the dumbbells, under control, to starting position in same groove.

Note: You can do the same exercise standing with knees slightly bent.

SEATED ALTERNATING DUMBBELL CURLS

1. Sit on end of a bench, torso straight, with arms straight at your sides, palms facing in, and feet on the floor.

2. Curl dumbbell past the thigh; then pronate (palm-up grip) to finishing position in front of shoulder. Don't swing weights up; keep elbows in at your sides.

3. Lower the dumbbell, under control, in same groove to starting position.

4. Repeat with the other arm, alternating reps until set is complete.

STANDING CURL BAR CURLS

1. Assume a hip-width stance with legs slightly bent, hands on outside angle on curl bar with arms straight and bar resting on the thighs.

2. Curl bar up, keeping elbows in at sides until hands are in front of shoulders at the top. Don't swing the bar up or let elbows turn out.

3. Slowly lower the bar in the same groove to starting position.

Chapter 5

STRENGTH-TRAINING PROGRAMS

strength-training program should be designed for the individual athlete, not a whole team. Each program should address strengths, weaknesses, priorities, needs, and target areas specific to the player. We can't prescribe individual programs for you because we don't know all these things about you. But we can show you three programs with options that would fit the needs of almost every athlete, regardless of sex, age, ability, or experience.

These programs use functional exercises for basketball that will improve proper muscle balance, thus increasing movement efficiency and reducing injuries. Each program has one to three recovery days between workouts. Research shows that the best recovery time for muscle repair and replenishment is 48 to 96 hours (depending on many variables).

Basic Fitness Program

The first program, basic fitness, is designed as a starting point. It's particularly effective for out-of-shape, beginning, and younger athletes. The program emphasizes body-weight-resistance exercises for developing muscular strength and endurance. You can do many of these exercises without weight equipment or weight machines.

Do this program three times a week (Monday, Wednesday, and Friday, or Tuesday, Thursday, and Saturday). Or you can do it two times a week (Monday and Thursday, or Tuesday and Friday). You can do one to three sets of each exercise, as your fitness level dictates. See table 5-1.

Table 5-1
Basic Fitness Program

1. Push-ups	1-3 sets × maximum repetitions	
2. Pull-ups	1-3 sets × maximum repetitions	
3. Bar dips	1-3 sets × maximum repetitions	
4. Step-ups	1-3 sets × 10-15 repetitions each leg	
5. Lunges	1-3 sets × 10-15 repetitions each leg	
6. Back extensions	1-3 sets × maximum—20 repetitions	
7. Abdominal crunches	1-3 sets × maximum—50 repetitions	
8. Leg raises	1-3 sets × maximum—50 repetitions	

Three-Day Total-Body Program

We designed this program for the beginning, intermediate, or advanced player who has only three days a week to lift weights. You may do this program Monday, Wednesday, and Friday, or Tuesday, Thursday, and Saturday, depending on your schedule. Allow one day of recovery between workouts. Wednesday's session works the same muscle groups as the Monday and Friday sessions but uses different optional exercises. See table 5-2.

You may start on either the upper or lower body. Whichever you decide to exercise first, finish that body segment completely before starting the exercises for the second body segment. Each session takes a little longer because you work the entire body in each workout. You may speed up the program by super setting two exercises at the same time. Super setting is performing two or more exercises one after the other before a rest period is taken; a super set can be performed with exercises for opposing muscle groups. Super setting is explained further under the four-day split program and under "Workout Cards" on page 120.

Table 5-2 Three-Day Total-Body Program	
Monday and Friday or Tuesday and Saturday	**Wednesday or Thursday**
1. Bench press	1. Incline bench press
2. Lat pull down	2. Lat row
3. Shoulder/Military press	3. Upright row/Lateral DB raises
4. Curl bar curls	4. Dumbbell curls
5. Bar dips	5. Tricep press downs
6. Squats/Leg press	6. Step-ups + Front and side lunges. 2 × each exercise
7. Power clean	7. Clean pull
8. Lying hamstring curls	8. Single leg hamstring curls
9. Standing heel raises	9. Single foot heel raises
10. Back extensions	10. Straight leg dead lift
11. Abdominal crunches	11. Leg raises

Note: On Monday and Friday or Tuesday and Saturday, if possible, do abduction-adduction exercises.

Sets and repetitions are listed in the sample 12-week off-season weight-training cycle for this program. See table 5-6.

Four-Day Split Program

This program (see table 5-3) may be used by the beginning, intermediate, or advanced athlete. This design allows a two- to three-day recovery time between the same muscle groups and allows you to focus on one body segment per workout—upper body or lower body. The workouts may be shorter depending on whether you super-set and on how many exercises you perform.

The workout days are Monday and Thursday for one body segment and Tuesday and Friday for the other. You may choose what days (Monday, Thursday, or Tuesday, Friday) to do either upper body or lower body programs.

This workout plan is also forgiving. If you miss a day, you should still have enough open days to do all your workouts. This workout is designed to super-set (do set number 1 of each exercise before progressing to set number 2 of each exercise) the exercises with the same number on the workout cards, which is explained on page 120. These exercises most often use opposing muscle groups or exercises that will not interfere with each other but will enhance each other. Some advantages of super setting include

1. faster workouts;
2. proper muscle balance;
3. increased conditioning levels;

Table 5-3
Four-Day Split Program

Lower body: Monday and Thursday	Upper body: Tuesday and Friday
1. Squat, hip sled, or leg press	1. Bench press: bar, dumbbell, or machine
1. Lying hamstring curls	1. Pull-ups or lat pull downs
2. Power cleans or clean pulls	2. Incline bench press: bar, dumbbell, or machine
	2. Lat row: machine, pulley, dumbbell, or T-bar
3. Step-ups, lunges, or leg extensions	3. Shoulder press: bar or dumbbell, seated or standing
3. Single leg, seated or standing hamstring curls	3. Upright row, lateral DB raises or shoulder fly machine
4. Side lunges or abduction-adduction exercises	4. Bar dips or tricep press downs
4. Standing calves or heel raises	4. Bicep curls: seated or standing, bar or dumbbell
5. Back extensions or straight leg dead lift	5. Abdominal crunches
5. Hanging leg raises: straight, bent, and sides	

4. a cleaner neuromuscular signal, recruitment, and function; and

5. increased blood flow to body segments being exercised.

Sets and repetitions are listed on the sample 12-week off-season weight-training cycle for this program.

STRENGTH-TRAINING PROGRESSION

Table 5-4 presents the five major phases of progression for weight training, the sets and reps for each phase, and the volume and intensity for each phase.

Table 5-4
Weight Training Phases of Progression

	PHASE				
	Hypertrophy	**Basic strength**	**Strength and power**	**Maintenance**	**Active rest**
Sets	3-4	3-4	3-4	3	1-2
Reps	8-12	4-6	2-3	10-8-6	15-20
Intensity	low	high	high	moderate	low
Volume	high	moderate	low	moderate	high

Does not include warm-up sets; target sets only.

The hypertrophy phase (hypertrophy is the increase in muscle tissue as a result of specific physiological adaptations from training) is important because it prepares you in two major ways for the higher-intensity phases to come later in the cycle. First, increases in muscle tissue improve your chances of developing strength and power. Second, your anaerobic capacity, or specific endurance related to weight-room exercises and workouts, will improve. This will help you in the later phases of the training cycle, allowing you to better handle the higher intensities.

The basic strength phase is a stage of increased strength for all major lifts. You begin training at higher intensities as increases in both strength and intensity will prepare you for the strength and power phase.

The strength and power phase has high intensity and lower volume. By reducing reps and focusing on target sets, you'll experience less fatigue but become stronger and more powerful. You might think of this as a peaking phase.

The maintenance or in-season phase is designed to retain as much of the strength and power achieved in the off-season program throughout the competitive season as is possible. You can modify the in-season maintenance program as circumstances or goals change.

Everyone agrees that during the competitive season athletes should reduce the frequency and intensity of strength-training workouts. Most in-season programs cut back on the number of exercises per body segment, usually using one ex-

Jason Kidd is in the starting position to perform a straight leg dead lift.

ercise per muscle group. These programs may do the total body each workout but with fewer exercises and fewer potential lifting days. On lighter lifting days you can substitute exercises (squats to leg extensions, step-ups, or hip sled; cleans to straight-leg deads or back extensions; bench press to machine or dumbbell bench).

During the season try to schedule two weight workouts per body part each week. If you have two days or more before the next game, you may lift heavier, using the 10-8-6 set repetitions recommended in this book. If you have only one day off between games, you may lift lighter, following the same 10-8-6, or you may do 15-12-10, 3 × 10, and so forth. Depending on game, practice, and travel schedules, you may have time for only one lower-body workout a week.

You should adjust or eliminate high-risk or certain technique lifts during the season to avoid overtraining, which may lead to decreased performance or injury.

Table 5-5 presents an in-season program with options. The sets and repetitions represent a heavier quality day of the in-season weight workout. Lighter day workout repetitions may be 15-12-10, 3 × 10, light 10-8-6, and so forth.

Table 5-5
In-Season Program

UPPER BODY

Muscle group	Exercise	Repetitions
Chest	Bench or incline; bar, machine, or dumbbell	10-8-6
Back	Pull-ups, lat pulldowns, pullovers, or rows	3 × max pullups 10-8-6
Shoulders	Machine or dumbbell shoulder flies, upright rows; bar or dumbbell	3 × 10
Biceps	Curl bar or dumbbell curls	10-8-6
Triceps	Tricep press down, tricep extension/press or bar dips	3 × 10
Abdominals	(See chapter 4 abdominal workout)	6 × 30-50

LOWER BODY

Muscle group	Exercise	Repetitions
Total body	Power cleans or clean pulls (may do once a week)	3 × 5
Quadriceps	Squats, hip sled, leg extensions, or step-ups	10-8-6
Hamstrings	Lying, seated, or standing	10-8-6
Groin and lateral hip	Abduction-adduction machine, pulley, or tubing (optional or one day a week)	2 × 10-15
Lower back	Straight leg dead lifts or back extension (may substitute for cleans once a week)	2 × 10-15
Abs and hip flexors	Hanging leg raises: straight, sides, knee-ups	2 × 10-20

The active rest phase is a postseason period of two to eight weeks immediately following the last game of the season. The length will vary depending on your situation. During active rest the body and mind should recover from the stresses you place on them during the season. Activities should be low in intensity and high in volume to allow the body to recover while still being somewhat active. Two light workouts a week with one or two sets of 15 to 20 repetitions per exercise should be about right. Circuit workouts are an option. It's also a good idea to do some cross training in other sports during active rest, but keep the intensity of the activity low for recovery purposes.

Twelve-Week Off-Season Strength-Training Program

The 12-week off-season cycle matches your workout cards except that it has the number of weeks listed at the top of the columns of the prescribed sets and repetitions for each exercise. See table 5-6. Certain exercises will have high school repetitions indicated by "H.S." for that exercise. If you're college age or older, you may follow the non-H.S. designated set and repetitions. If you're younger than high school age, refer to "prepubescent weight training" in the Glossary for sets and repetitions.

On the major lifts—squat, leg press, power clean, bench press, incline press, and so forth—the sets and repetitions prescribed include target sets only. They don't include warm-up sets. In target sets, use the heaviest weight possible while maintaining proper technique and performing all the prescribed repetitions in a set.

If the 12-week off-season cycle is your program, please follow all of it the way it was designed for best results in the three-day and four-day split programs.

Basic fitness and in-season programs are listed earlier in this chapter and are different from the 12-week off-season cycle program workout cards.

Kenny Anderson demonstrates the power clean.

Table 5-6
Twelve-Week Off-Season Cycle

UPPER BODY

Exercises	3 Weeks	2 Weeks	4 Weeks	2 Weeks	1 Week	2 Weeks
1. Bench press (bar, dumbbell, or machine)	4 × 10 quality sets	4 × 8 quality sets	4 × 6 quality sets	College 5-3-2-2 H.S. 4 × 6 quality sets	College 6-4-3-2 H.S. 4 × 6 quality sets	College 5-3-2-2 H.S. 4 × 6 quality sets
1. Pronated grip pull-ups/ pull-downs (wide behind head, shoulder width in front)	4 × maximum or 4 × 10	4 × maximum or 4 × 8 weighted	4 × maximum or 10-8-6-10 weighted	4 × maximum or 10-8-6-10 weighted	4 × maximum or 10-8-6-10 weighted	
2. Incline bench press (bar, dumbbell, or machine)	4 × 10 quality sets	4 × 8 quality sets	4 × 6 quality sets	College 5-3-2-2 H.S. 4 × 6 quality sets	College 6-4-3-2 H.S. 4 × 6 quality sets	
2. Seated lat row or dumbbell lat row, or T-bar	4 × 10	4 × 8	10-8-8-6	10-8-8-6	10-8-6	
3. Military press or shoulder push press (bar, dumbbell, machine, standing or seated)	3 × 10 quality sets	3 × 8 quality sets	10-8-6	10-8-6	10-8-6	
3. Upright row, shrugs, dumbbell raises, shoulder fly machine	3 × 10	3 × 10	10-8-8	10-8-8	10-8-10	
4. Tricep extension/ press, bar dips, tricep press downs	3-4 × maximum or 3-4 × 10 weighted	3-4 × maximum or 3-4 × 8 weighted	3-4 × maximum or 10-8-6 weighted	3-4 × maximum or 10-8-6 weighted	3-4 × maximum or 10-8-6 weighted	
4. Bicep curls (bar or dumbbells)	3-4 × 10	10-10-8-8	10-8-6-6	10-8-6-6	10-8-6-6	
5. Abdominal crunches: straight, bent, and rotary	30-40 reps each	30-40 reps each	30-40 reps each	30-40 reps each	30-40 reps each	

Table 5-6
(continued)

LOWER BODY

Exercises	3 Weeks	2 Weeks	4 Weeks	1 Week	2 Weeks
1. Squats/leg press	4 × 10 quality sets	4 × 8 quality sets	4 × 6 quality sets	College 6-4-3-2 H.S. 4 × 6 quality sets	College 5-3-2-2 H.S. 4 × 6 quality sets
1. Lying hamstring curls	4 × 10	4 × 10	10-10-8-8	10-8-6-6	10-8-6-6
2. Clean pulls or power cleans	8-6-6-6 quality sets	H.S. 8-6-6-6 8-6-6-4 quality sets	H.S. 8-5-5-5 8-5-5-4 quality sets	H.S. 8-5-5-5 6-4-3-2 quality sets	H.S. 8-5-5-5 6-4-3-2 quality sets
3. Step-ups, lunges, or leg extensions	3 × 10	3 × 10	3 × 10	10-8-8	10-8-6
3. Hamstring curls (seated, single leg, or standing)	3 × 10	3 × 10	3 × 10	10-8-8	10-8-6
4. Side lunge or adductors-abductors	2 × 12-15	2 × 12-15	2 × 12-15	2 × 12-15	2 × 12-15
4. Three-way standing calves or heel raises	2 × 15-25 each way	2 × 15-25 each way	2 × 15-25 each way	2 × 15-25 each way	2 × 15-25 each way
5. Back extensions or straight leg dead lifts	3 × 10-15	3 × 10-15	3 × 10-15	3 × 10-15	3 × 10-15
5. Hanging leg raises Bent Straight Sides	2 × 15-30 2 × 10-15 2 × 15-25	2 × 15-30 2 × 10-15 2 × 15-25	2 × 15-30 2 × 10-15 2 × 15-25	2 × 15-30 2 × 10-15 2 × 15-25	2 × 15-30 2 × 10-15 2 × 15-25

WORKOUT CARDS

The blank workout cards match the basic fitness program (chart 5-1a) and the 12-week off-season cycle (charts 5-1b and 5-1c). Make 5 to 10 copies of the blank workout cards and always keep a blank master for future copying needs. The numbers on the card represent the exercises that you should do together if super setting, which we explain below.

BENCH PRESS	100 × 15
	135 × 10
	155 × 8
	185 × 6

Super setting means that you do set number 1 of each exercise (as shown on the workout cards) before progressing to set number 2 of each exercise. Continue this alternating pattern for the prescribed sets or repetitions for each of the exercises super setted throughout the program.

At the top of the card you have a place for your name, and in each daily column you have a place for your body weight and the date. In the small boxes next to each exercise, list your sets and repetitions.

List the weight first and then your repetitions; the top box is the first set, the second box is the second set, and so on.

Each card or chart has exercise options for most numbers to fit your specific needs: facilities, equipment, favorite exercises, physical limitations, and so forth.

If you follow the numbers and prescribed sets and repetitions, you'll have a functional program that increases performance and reduces the chance of injury.

Chart 5-1a
Workout Cards

BASIC FITNESS PROGRAM

Name:

Body weight:

Date:

Exercises	Reps:																		
Push-ups																			
Pull-ups																			
Bar dips																			
Step-ups																			
Lunges																			
Back extensions																			
Abdominal crunches																			
Leg raises																			

Chart 5-1b
Workout Cards

UPPER BODY

Name:

Body weight:

Exercises	Date:																						
	Reps:																						
1. Bench press (bar, dumbbell, or machine)																							
1. Pronated grip pull-ups, pull-downs (wide behind head, shoulder width in front)																							
2. Incline bench press (bar, dumbbell, or machine)																							
2. Seated lat row or dumbbell lat row or T-bar																							
3. Military press or shoulder push press (bar or dumbbell, seated or stand)																							
3. Upright row, shrugs or dumbbell lateral raises, shoulder fly machine																							
4. Tricep extension/press, bar dips, tricep press downs																							
4. Bicep curls (bar or dumbbells)																							
5. Abdominal crunches: Straight / Bent / Rotary																							

Chart 5-1c
Workout Cards

LOWER BODY

Name:

Body weight:

Exercises	Date:																											
	Reps:																											
1. Squats/leg press																												
1. Lying hamstring curls																												
2. Clean pulls or power cleans																												
3. Step-ups, lunges, or leg extensions																												
3. Hamstring curls (seated, single leg, or standing)																												
4. Side lunges or adductors-abductors 12-15																												
4. Heel raises or 3-way standing calves 15-25																												
5. Back extensions or straight leg dead lifts 10-15																												
5. Hanging leg raises: Straight, Bent, Sides																												

PART

III

Power
in Motion

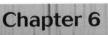

PLYOMETRIC TRAINING

ou've probably heard of plyometrics, but you may not know exactly what it is. Plyometrics involves exercises that put your muscles on a rapid pre-stretch before an explosive contraction. Plyometric exercises include jumps, bounds, power skips, and hops. Plyometric training is demanding on the body, but the results on the court are worth it.

POWER FORMULA

The ability to generate power is critical to successful athletic performance. And power is particularly important in basketball, in which jumping and exploding quickly for the ball are key performance factors.

Power is the relationship between strength (force) and speed, or, more precisely

$$POWER = \frac{FORCE \times DISTANCE}{TIME}$$

Strength, or force, is a major component of power. But what kind of strength? It's not the number of pounds you can lift in the weight room, which we call absolute strength. Absolute strength is of little value to a basketball player if it's not transferable to the dynamic demands of the sport.

A powerful player is able to generate maximum force in the shortest time possible. Power, therefore, is the ability to exert force explosively. This force may involve

- the timely contraction of the muscles that extend the ankles, knees, hips, back, and shoulders just before a vertical jump; or
- the force generated by a coordinated contraction of the chest, shoulders, and triceps during a basketball chest pass.

Vertical and horizontal jumping are power activities. To improve your vertical jump, you should first strengthen the specific muscles involved in the movement. For example, the major muscles involved in vertical jumping include the calves, hamstrings, gluteals, quadriceps, and shoulders (strong abdominal and low-back muscles are also important).

Possessing strength is only part of the total picture. Jumping improves jumping. To improve your vertical jump, practice vertical jumping. Combine the drills presented later in this chapter with the strength-training programs in part II and you'll see significant gains in your vertical-jumping ability.

PLYOMETRIC MOVEMENTS

The position of every basketball player on the floor changes from moment to moment. As a result, you must continually adjust to fit each circumstance. Forward, backward, lateral, and vertical movements involving sprints, shuffles, slides, skips, and hops are several of the many actions you may perform in a

Clifford Robinson shows his power while exploding for a dunk.

© NBA Photos/Glenn James

typical basketball game. Your conditioning program should focus on developing the skills and power to execute these movements at a high level.

You can design plyometric drills based on your individual needs. You may use drills that closely resemble movement patterns unique to your position and style of play. You might also incorporate basic movement patterns found in most sports, such as lateral, forward, backward, vertical, and rotational movements, and combinations thereof. For example, if you have difficulty moving quickly to your left and right, you might benefit from drills that emphasize explosive lateral movements.

The number of plyometric drills available is limited only by the possible movements an athlete can perform and the imagination required to develop them. Try to create drills to accommodate the situations you face in games. Variety will help prevent boredom and burnout, and help you address any weaknesses that might develop from performing the same drills repeatedly. When creating new drills, proceed with caution. Try the exercises at half or three-quarter speed first before you go full-steam ahead.

SAFETY CONSIDERATIONS FOR PLYOMETRICS

Plyometric training is not for every athlete, especially the underconditioned athlete. The exercises and degree of difficulty you choose must be right for your body. Don't compare your exercises and their difficulty with those being performed by more advanced athletes.

Consult your physician and coach before beginning plyometric training. If you have a history of injuries or are currently recovering from an injury, you should stay away from plyometrics. Only after obtaining a doctor's or trainer's release should an injured athlete resume plyometric conditioning.

Surface

The surface on which you perform plyometrics should be semiresilient. Good surfaces include a properly built basketball court, a tumbling mat, a rubberized track, and dry, well-groomed grass.

Footwear

Always wear shoes, preferably basketball shoes. They provide good lateral stability, heel cushioning, arch support, and nonslip soles.

Equipment

Boxes should be strong and sturdy, without protruding objects such as handles on the top or sides. Boxes should vary in height from three inches to three feet. Cover the box with a smooth, not shaggy, carpet. Glue the carpet to the box. The carpet should give the box some padding but not slow your movement; it shouldn't create much friction on the bottom of your shoe.

Muggsy Bogues prepares to do a box jump

Don't cover the box with rubber matting. It may feel soft under your foot, but your rubber sole will tend to stick to the rubber matting at the moment you try to jump. Some drills require a slight twisting action. If you try to twist or pivot while in contact with a rubber-topped box, a joint injury could occur.

Barriers

Barriers should never be the cause of an injury. Foam barriers or a couple of rolled-up towels with a piece of tape wrapped around them work well.

Medicine Balls

Medicine balls are extremely useful for upper- and lower-body plyometrics. Inflatable rubber medicine balls work best because they rebound when they hit the floor or wall. Medicine balls should weigh from 2 to 15 pounds.

Spotting

As the drills become more advanced or as the athlete becomes fatigued, it's important that at least one person stand ready to spot potential problems before an injury occurs. Other athletes turn out to be the best spotters because they know the early warning signs of exhaustion. Spotting should be taught as an integral part of athletes' plyometric training.

Age

Young athletes—even first-year high school students, for example—should be especially careful and strictly supervised when performing plyometrics. Young athletes are more likely to injure a joint or damage a growth plate in the bones. Therefore, they should perform only those exercises that we label "low intensity" and "low impact" in this book.

Intensity

You should approach a plyometric workout with caution. Just because an exercise looks easy doesn't mean that it *is* easy. You should work from the less difficult plyometric exercises to the more advanced drills. That way your body will adapt in the most efficient manner.

More is not always better. We are more concerned with the speed of the jump than the height of the drop. This is true because the risk of injury far outweighs the potential for physical improvement. We frequently perform several tests on the players (vertical jump, horizontal jump, agility sprint). And we continually see improvements in our test results and on the court.

SIX GUIDELINES FOR PLYOMETRICS

Here are a half-dozen keys to using plyometrics correctly in your conditioning program.

1. Develop a strength base first. It's very important that you understand your level of strength before you begin a plyometric program. Sufficient strength is critical because it will permit you to use the correct drill technique and thereby reduce the risk of injury. Coaches can assess strength improvements by continual observation and selected standards of measurement. These can indicate whether or not you are ready to advance to the next level of drill difficulty.

Plyometrics is best employed when combined with a strength-training program. These drills are not a replacement for a strength regimen. Remember, power is the relationship between strength and speed. Therefore, the stronger the athlete, the greater the potential for increased power development. As your strength levels improve, you may progress to higher intensity drills.

Plyometric exercises help Kevin Garnett perform explosive movements like this dunk.

© NBA Photos/Scott Cunningham

2. Always remember to warm up, stretch, and cool down. As you know from chapter 1 and your experience, warm-up, stretching, and cool-down are essential parts of a conditioning program. Calisthenics and low-intensity skipping are examples of warm-up activities.

Follow the active warm-up by a total-body stretching routine. After you have completed the plyometric training session, you should again perform some low-intensity active cool-down activities. Then finish the session with more stretching.

3. Schedule plyometrics for the early part of the workout. Athletes typically perform plyometrics, like other high-intensity activities, immediately following the warm-up and before other exercises scheduled for that training session. Since the training focus of plyometrics is neuromuscular, fatigue can have a negative impact, especially for the lesser-developed athlete. Therefore, you should perform plyometrics at highest intensity when you are fresh. This will also decrease the chance of injury.

Discontinue a plyometric exercise or drill when you reach a point of moderate fatigue. Always maintain proper technique to achieve maximum gain and decrease chance of injury. Get adequate rest between sets and sessions to allow your body time to recover and ultimately adapt to the physical stress imposed.

4. Perform plyometrics at the correct intensity. When performing plyometrics, you should be mindful of the purpose of the drill and the technique required. The degree of impact within a particular drill determines intensity levels. The following exercises are generally categorized as high-intensity plyometrics:

- Single-leg hops for distance
- Depth jumps from tall boxes
- Bounding
- High-barrier jumps

Conversely, these exercises could be called low-intensity plyometrics:

- Double-leg jumps in place
- Running in place
- Skipping rope
- Side-to-side jumps over a small barrier

The beginner should establish solid technique before advancing to higher-intensity plyometrics. Drill intensity will vary depending on your physical makeup. For example, the amount of impact—and therefore the intensity level—would be significantly greater for a 200-pound athlete performing a simple depth jump off a 12-inch box than the same drill performed by a 130-pound athlete (both being beginning athletes).

CONDITIONING TIP

When performing repetitive jumping drills, as you attain your peak height and begin your descent, start thinking about the next jump before hitting the ground. Flex your elbows, shoulders, hips, and knees to be ready for the next jump.

5. Progress gradually from easy to more difficult plyometrics. Exercise difficulty is closely associated with intensity. Many drills and exercises appear to be easy and have a low intensity. It is in these exercises that you must take special care not to overindulge.

Plyometrics are extremely demanding on your body, so you should carefully follow a program that gradually progresses from beginning to advanced exercises. Beginners should build a base by performing flat-surfaced, double-leg, and low-impact drills. Once you develop a strength base, you can incorporate into your program more demanding exercises such as single-leg, tall-barrier, and higher-impact drills.

6. Adjust the number of repetitions, sets, and workouts as appropriate. How many reps and sets you perform depends on the intensity of the drill. Generally, a low-intensity exercise would require a higher number of repetitions. Conversely, an exercise with a higher degree of difficulty would call for fewer repetitions.

Do not exceed six high-impact exercises during any plyometric workout. The total volume of repetitions will be determined by the number of exercises you perform, the number of sets per drill, and the degree of difficulty. For full recovery of your muscles, tendons, and ligaments, allow a two- or three-day rest period (48-hour minimum) between sessions.

Tom Gugliotta works on proper skipping techniqe.

PLYOMETRIC PROGRAMS

Starting Plyometric Training

Length

- 12 weeks
- One to two sessions per week
- 15 to 30 minutes per session

Recovery

- 48 to 72 hours minimum between sessions
- Two to four minutes between sets

Reps/sets

- 80 to 120 total repetitions per upper or lower body per session

Intensity

- Low

In-Season Plyometric Training

Length

- Varies depending on the length of the season, competition schedule, practice intensity, and minutes played during a game
- One to two sessions per week
- 15 to 30 minutes per session

Recovery

- 48 hours minimum between sessions
- One to three minutes between sets

Reps/sets

- Repetitions per upper or lower body per session for novice athlete: 25 to 75 repetitions
- Repetitions per upper or lower body per session for mature athlete: 50 to 100 repetitions

Intensity

- Low to moderate

Note: In-season plyometrics training is to be done by athletes not getting much playing time. Be careful not to overtrain.

Postseason Plyometric Training

Length

- Start four weeks after the end of the in-season
- Lasts four weeks

Recovery

- Time should be spent in "active rest" type activities

Reps/sets and intensity

- Intensity, frequency, and duration of training sessions drop considerably

Off-Season Plyometric Training

Length

- Varies depending upon competition schedule, although ideally 12 weeks
- Two to three sessions per week
- 30 to 45 minutes per session

Recovery

- 48 hours minimum between sessions
- One to two minutes between sets

Reps/sets

- Total repetitions per upper or lower body per session for novice athlete: 100 to 150 repetitions
- Total repetitions per upper or lower body per session for mature athlete: 150 to 200 repetitions

Intensity

- Moderate to high

PLYOMETRIC DRILLS

Before starting your routine, carefully pick the movement patterns you need. Concentrate on drills that are right for you. Make sure you perform the basic movements well before tackling harder ones.

The drills that follow are some of the more popular ones developed for basketball players. This is only a small sample of the many plyometric exercises you might do. Once you catch on, we encourage you to create your own drills.

Note: One repetition equals one full completion of the exercise. For example, if you perform a simple jump in place, each time your feet touch the floor, count one repetition. If an exercise requires multiple movements, such as side-to-side barrier jumps, count one "round trip" (that is, over and back) as one repetition.

RIM JUMPS

As the name implies, you jump up and try to touch the rim. If you can't reach the rim, then try to get as high as the bottom of the backboard, the net, or any other suspended object. This drill is a series of rapid vertical jumps. You should concentrate on being quick off the ground. A good phrase to remember is "touch and go."

The speed of the jump is more important than the height; however, always encourage yourself to make maximum vertical effort.

1. Assume an upright stance, eyes focused on the target.
2. Start by quickly dropping to a quarter-squat position—flex ankles, knees, hips, shoulders, and elbows.
3. Immediately jump and reach to the target (with one hand).

KNEES TO ELBOWS

Like the rim jump, this drill requires you to jump to maximum height with your hips and knees flexed during the flight phase, while maintaining quickness off the ground. The difference is that your eyes stay focused straight ahead or slightly down.

1. Perform this drill in a series of rapid vertical jumps.
2. Stand in an upright and balanced position.
3. Quickly drop to a quarter-squat position—flex ankles, knees, hips, shoulders, and elbows.
4. Immediately jump and simultaneously drive your knees to your elbows (arm position is horizontal to the ground).

BARRIER JUMPS: FORWARD AND BACKWARD

By putting into play an obstacle like a small foam barrier, rolled-up towel, or collapsible hurdle, you now have a visual cue about how high you need to jump. You can vary the height of the barrier, use more than one barrier, or alter the distance between barriers. Using a number of barriers will allow you to vary your stride length or jump length.

Emphasize the speed of the jumps because you know the height of the jumps. Besides developing speed and quickness, this drill will improve your agility and foot speed.

You need only one barrier initially, but after you've mastered one barrier, try the drill with two or three barriers.

1. To begin, select a barrier that is six inches or less in height and width (as your technique and strength improve, you can increase the height of the barrier).

2. Stand in a balanced, upright position, eyes focused on the approximate landing spot for your first jump.

3. Keep your feet together, with your toes a couple of inches from the barrier.

4. Slightly flex your shoulders and elbows so they are ready to assist in the jump. Don't let your arms drop from this position during the drill.

5. Jump forward over the barrier. Jump high and far enough so your heels clear the barrier. Keep your toes pointing straight ahead; don't let your feet turn to one side (a common mistake).

6. Immediately reverse the jump. Maintain your body control and jump back-ward to the initial starting position. Continue until you complete the set.

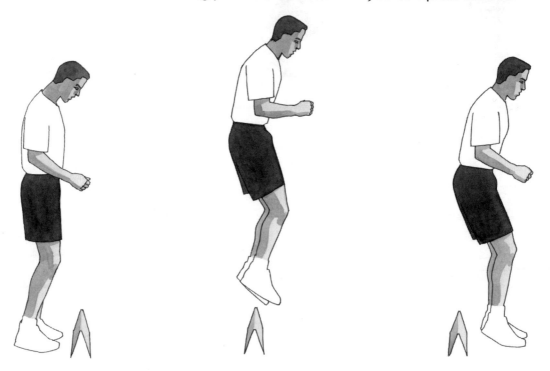

BARRIER JUMPS: SIDE TO SIDE

Basketball requires the ability to move laterally quickly, explosively, and efficiently. The following drill specifically trains the adductors and abductors of the thighs, legs, and feet, which are important muscles for lateral movement.

1. Select a barrier that is six inches or less in height and width. (As technique and strength levels improve, you can increase the height of the barrier.)

2. Stand in an upright position, eyes focused on the approximate landing spot for your first jump.

3. Place your feet together and parallel to the barrier. Your feet should be a comfortable distance from the side of the barrier. Remember, the barrier is at your side.

4. Jump sideways over the barrier and land in the same ready position, prepared to make the next jump.

5. Immediately repeat the jump in the opposite direction. Don't stop between side-to-side jumps until you complete the set.

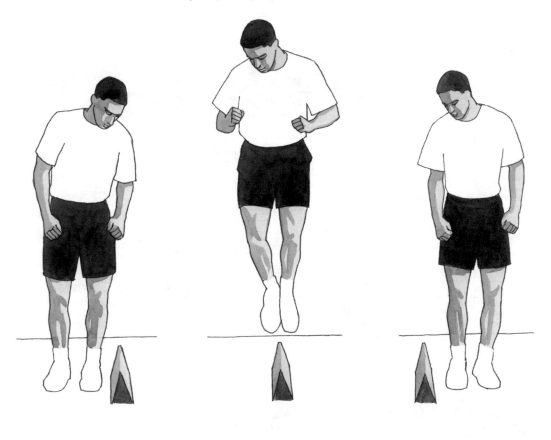

BOX JUMPS: UP AND DOWN REPEATS—FORWARD

The next four drills require a box approximately 9 to 12 inches in height. The best width for a box is 24 inches, and the length should be 36 inches. If there's no box available, a stair step would work for this drill.

Box drills require you to raise your entire body weight the height of the box. You must then be able to control the impact of your body weight combined with the force of gravity upon landing. As in all types of jumping, speed off the ground is critical.

1. Stand on the box with your feet together. Your heels should be hanging over the edge.

2. Slightly extend your shoulders and flex your elbows so they are ready to assist in the jump.

3. Drop, don't jump, off the box.

4. Upon contact with the ground, immediately jump back up to the starting position. Concentrate on quickness. Your heels shouldn't touch the ground.

BOX JUMPS: UP AND DOWN REPEATS—LATERAL

All professional basketball players know the importance of mastering explosive lateral movements. Such moves are valuable, especially on defense. This is an excellent drill for promoting lateral power.

1. Stand on the box with your feet parallel to each other and close to the edge.

2. Slightly extend your shoulders and flex your elbows so they're ready to assist in the jump.

3. Drop laterally off the box. Make sure the drop is far enough away from the box to avoid catching your foot or ankle on the edge.

4. When you reach the ground, immediately jump back up to your starting position. Try to do a touch-and-go action with the ground. In many cases, your heels will not touch down.

LATERAL BOX SHUFFLE

This is a tremendous drill for developing lateral movement and agility. This plyometric exercise works best when you use a short box (9 inches or less). Be sure to shuffle across the narrow width—24 inches—of the box.

Speed is important, but safety is critical. Therefore, make sure you have enough clearance between your foot and the edge of the box. Don't perform this drill if you become fatigued.

1. Stand next to the box with your outside foot on the floor and the other foot positioned on top and in the middle of the box.
2. Focus your eyes on the box.
3. Hold your arms in the defensive ready position.
4. Lift up slightly with the leg positioned on the box and quickly shift your weight across to the other side, keeping your center of gravity low.
5. After crossing the box, your feet should make contact simultaneously (that is, the "ground foot" and the "box foot" should land at the same time).
6. Immediately repeat in the opposite direction.

BOX-DROP JUMP SHOT

This a great drill for developing your vertical jump while at the same time performing a basketball skill such as catching and shooting. This exercise will challenge your coordination, agility, and power.

1. Position a box within your shooting range.
2. Stand on the floor behind the box facing the basket.
3. A coach or partner, holding a ball, takes position between the box and the basket.

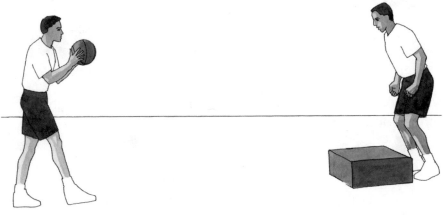

4. Jump with both feet onto the box and quickly drop down to the floor on the other side.

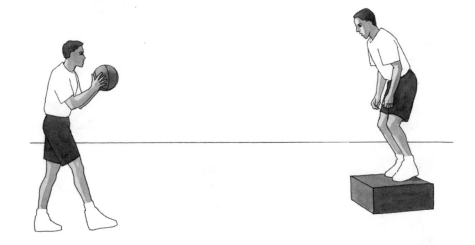

5. The coach or partner passes the ball sometime between the start of your first jump and the landing on the opposite side of the box. Catch the ball before landing on the floor.

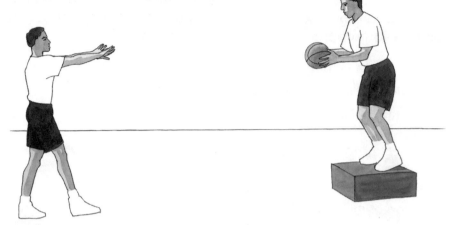

6. When you land, immediately and explosively jump as high as you can and shoot a jump shot.

7. After the shot, the coach or partner rebounds the ball while you prepare for the next repetition.

MEDICINE-BALL TOSS

You can do this drill using either a single-arm toss (1- to 4-pound ball) or a double-arm toss (4- to 12-pound ball). We describe a double-arm toss in this example. This drill will develop upper-body power.

1. Stand three to four feet from a solid wall, feet shoulder-width apart.
2. Grasp a rubber medicine ball on both sides. Now raise the ball over your head, with your elbows flexed to a 45- to 90-degree angle and your thumbs pointing down.
3. Extend your elbows explosively, and the ball will fly hard against the wall. Be sure to aim slightly higher than your hands at the point of the ball's release.
4. When the ball rebounds back, you should fully extend your arms as you catch it. The momentum of the ball will drive your arms back to a position where the elbows are approximately at a 45- to 90-degree angle.
5. Immediately repeat this process. Do 15 to 50 repetitions per set.

MEDICINE-BALL SQUAT TOSS

The squat toss is an excellent drill for developing power in your legs and shoulder girdle.

A 6- to 12-pound medicine ball works best for this drill, but make sure you can control a lighter ball before advancing to a heavier one. Use correct throwing technique, getting your legs and hips involved. Never use your back to throw. The drill is designed to develop leg power, so make your leg muscles do most of the work.

1. Stand in a balanced and upright position, with your feet slightly wider than shoulder-width.
2. Hold the ball at arms' length.

3. Start by quickly dropping to a quarter-squat position—flex ankles, knees, and hips. Arms remain straight during the drop. Keep your back straight and tight.

4. Immediately drive your legs straight up as if jumping to the ceiling.

5. Start the momentum of the ball with your legs and continue the ball's movement by using your upper body and arms. At the instant you release the ball, you should fully extend your body.

6. Toss the ball as high as possible. Concentrate on making your legs and shoulder girdle perform the toss. If done correctly, you will jump into the throw.

7. Allow the ball to bounce off the ground. Retrieve it for subsequent tosses.

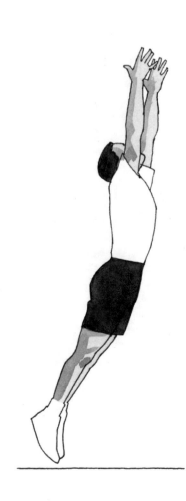

SPEED TRAINING

How fast are you? How long does it take for you to run from one end of the court to the other? Your speed is determined by the time it takes for you to move from point A to point B, say from one baseline to the other, running between 90 and 100 percent of your capacity.

Many people believe that a person is born with speed and can't be taught to run faster. This is simply not true. Athletes can be trained to sprint faster, just as singers can be taught to sing better. While you may not have the genetic makeup to run as fast as Michael Johnson, you *can* make a significant improvement in your present speed.

Speed is a great asset in basketball, because speed encompasses more than just sprinting straight ahead. The ability to move quickly and efficiently while changing directions, shuffling, or back pedaling is important on both ends of the court, whereas running speed is especially critical in the transition game, shifting from offense to defense and defense to offense.

The information and drills in this chapter will help you develop your speed to its potential.

Make the most of it so you are always a step ahead of your opponent.

Kevin Johnson uses his speed to get past his opponent.

© NBA Photos/Barry Gossage

SPEED FACTORS

What determines your speed? Whether running straight forward or straight backward, the two basic components of speed are

- stride length—the distance covered in a single step; and,
- stride frequency—the number of steps taken in a given unit of time.

The fastest runners have a high rate of arm and leg speed, a lengthy stride, or both. This is true for sprinters who run straight ahead, and it's true for athletes whose sport requires a high degree of lateral, backward, and combination movements. Many coaches consider sprinting to be the most fundamental of all athletic movements. The two basic components of speed are:

STRIDE FREQUENCY × STRIDE LENGTH

You can improve your stride frequency and stride length by increasing the force you produce from your arms and legs. You increase stride frequency by moving your arms and legs faster. Stride length is determined by the span from one foot to the other when they are farthest apart as you run.

You, like every athlete, have inherent limitations about how fast you can move your arms and legs (frequency) and the length of your stride. You can improve your speed, however, by producing a greater stride length and a faster stride frequency.

To improve your performance, learn the speed techniques taught in this chapter. They'll pay off throughout your competitive career.

SPRINTING TECHNIQUE

Stand up straight, with your shoulders, knees, hips, and ankles properly aligned. During the power phase of a sprint, your foot exerts a powerful push force to the ground, propelling your body forward.

As you begin running, your body will automatically shift into a slightly forward lean. Remember to keep your upper body in front of your belly button.

To ensure proper sprinting technique, you must achieve total balance and coordinate your limbs in a synchronized rhythm. Remember, sprinting is a rhythmic losing and gaining of your balance.

Use the following checklist to fully maximize your sprint potential:

1. Body alignment is critical. You should maintain proper alignment when you're sprinting and through the duration of the drills.

2. Keep your shoulders squared and relaxed, with no torso rotation.

3. Keep your elbows at a 90-degree angle. Don't let your angle change. Keep your elbows in, swinging loosely from your shoulders close to your body.

4. Keep your hands slightly open. They should go no higher than your shoulders on the forward swing and no farther back than your hips on the back swing.

5. Drive the knee of your drive leg in a straight line forward, not upward.

6. Fully extend your push leg (but do not overextend because that will cause you to fall out of balance and rhythm).

7. Keep your eyes focused straight ahead. Avoid head movement up, down, or to the side.

SPEED DEVELOPMENT

A fast player like Tim Hardaway moves smoothly, explosively, and effortlessly around the court, whereas others tend to lumber along or rush their actions at inappropriate times. So, while having speed and quickness is essential, knowing how and when to use it is just as important.

To increase his speed, Mitch Richmond works on a speed development drill.

Streamlining your movements and becoming faster isn't easy, but it is possible to become more efficient and explosive in your strides. You can do it by breaking the sprint action down and then practicing each part. When you reassemble the parts, your sprinting action will have greatly improved. By practicing each part of the whole movement you can more selectively enhance your strengths and eliminate your weaknesses.

Arm Movement Exercises

Speed is generated not only in the legs; the arms have much to do with how fast the legs go. So, to maximize your speed, you need to use your arms to their full advantage. Here are a few exercises to get you started.

ARM CIRCLES

1. To become more aware of the shoulder's function, consciously relax the muscles surrounding it. The shoulders are relaxed when they "let go" toward the ground rather than inch up toward the sky. Maintain this relaxation throughout this exercise.

2. Move your arms slowly in a circle. The circular movement will help you feel and understand more about your shoulder's movement capabilities. Now you're ready to try a couple more arm exercises.

ARM SWINGS

1. Swing your arms forward and then back alongside the body. Maintain relaxed shoulders while you swing your arms straight forward and back. Also, keep your hands and fingers loose and relaxed. Clenching your fists will create tension in your forearms and shoulders and thereby inhibit a free swinging movement at your shoulders.

2. Bend your elbows to 90 degrees, swinging them freely from the shoulder. Keep the arms moving forward and back but never raise your hands higher than chest or shoulder level or back past your hips.

3. As you progress in your practice, you can work on moving your arms faster while standing in place. Remember, arm speed helps your leg speed!

BONGOS

1. Sit on the floor or on a bench with your legs extended.
2. Pump your arms, bent 90 degrees at the elbow, as if you were hitting down on an imaginary bongo drum. The harder you beat down, the greater the opposite leg will push when running.

Remember to use proper arm action during each of the following exercises.

Leg Movement Exercises

ABCs IN RUNNING EXERCISES

The running stride can be broken down into three phases—knee lift, leg reach, and back-leg extension, or push-off. Back-leg extension or push-off is the synchronized extension of the hip, knee, or ankle joints involving the gluteals, hamstrings, and gastrocnemius. To keep things simple and in sequence, in the running exercises that follow we'll refer to these three phases as the ABCs, where

> A = Knee-lift exercises
> B = Leg reach
> C = Back-leg extension, bounding, or push-off

EXERCISE A1

1. March with the knees coming high and then down.
2. Emphasize staying on the balls of the feet and maintain a straight body alignment while your knee drives up.
3. Keep your thigh parallel to the ground while the opposite leg stays straight.
4. When your drive knee reaches its highest point (for example, thigh parallel to the ground), the ankle of the same leg should be dorsiflexed with the foot positioned directly under your knee.
5. Make sure you use proper arm action.

CONDITIONING TIP

A good way to work on body alignment is to keep your upper body in front of your belly button.

EXERCISE A2

Repeat exercise A1, except instead of marching, skip as you alternate legs.

EXERCISE A3

Perform exercise A1 running, emphasizing higher knee lift. Limit your stride length. As you move down the court (or field), take approximately three steps per yard. Emphasize proper body alignment with the hips positioned under your torso. This will help to ease you into a full range of motion and allow better leverage for a more explosive stride.

EXERCISE B1

1. Walk so as to drive the lead knee up.
2. Extend the leg at the knee joint.
3. Pull the leg back to the ground. The harder you pull back on the ground, the harder the ground will push back against your force. The back-pulling action ensures that the foot does not contact the ground too far in front of the body. Pulling will also prevent an undesirable vertical body position. Continually reinforce the action of leading with the knee (before extending your leg during the leg reach). Follow through by bringing your heel to your buttocks.

EXERCISE B2

Same as exercise B1 except include a skip between alternating legs.

EXERCISE B3

1. Similar to exercise B1, but emphasize high knee lift, good leg reach, and explosive gluteal and hamstring involvement (pull back on the ground and bring the heel up).
2. Move down the court slowly. Maintain proper body alignment, with your chest slightly in front of your body's center of gravity.
3. Contact the ground on the balls of your feet, not flat-footed.

CONDITIONING TIP

The ability to execute an explosive knee drive combined with an efficient leg reach will promote the development of a longer stride. The harder you pull back on the floor, the harder the floor pushes back in the same direction you are pulling.

EXERCISE C1

Hop using this foot movement pattern: right-right, left-left, right-right, and so on. The length of the hops is not as important as performing the correct technique:

- Focus on fully extending the back leg and attaining as much height as possible.
- Bring the lead leg up similar to the way you do the A exercises, trying to hop high in the air while extending the back leg and pushing up and back.

EXERCISE C2

1. Unlike the hopping drill, here you alternate the leg action: right-left-right-left and so on. Emphasis is on developing a full extension of the back, or push, leg. This exaggerated form of sprinting is called bounding.

2. During the knee-drive phase you'll notice a slight pause while you are in flight. You should achieve full extension of the hip and knee and plantar-flexion of the ankle during the push. Try to get as much distance as possible between bounds. This will force you to really extend the back leg.

ANKLE FLIPS

1. With knees slightly bent and body in perfect alignment (shoulder, hip, knee, and ankle in a straight line), get as high on the balls of the feet as possible.

2. Forcefully jump off of the balls of your feet in alternating fashion while jumping with slightly bent knees. Land on the balls of your feet, not flat-footed.

3. As the right foot pushes off, the left foot should slide above the floor surface.

CONDITIONING TIP

When performing running exercises, always maintain proper arm action. Stay high on the balls of your feet. Foot and ankle strength are vitally important for developing an explosive push-off.

HEEL KICKS

1. Run down the court alternately bringing your heels up, touching your buttocks.

2. Move down the court slowly.

3. Tap heel to buttocks as fast as you can, while still maintaining control.

Note: Please see page 23 for the heel kick figure.

Acceleration

We've explained and shown, in some detail, how to sprint properly. Now let's focus on developing your ability to accelerate.

How long does it take you to go from a stationary position to a full sprint? In basketball, the shorter the better. Consider the great fast-breaking teams and players you've seen. They have great acceleration and use it to their advantage on the court.

The following exercise sequence will help develop your ability to accelerate.

FOUR-STEP ACCELERATION DRILL

1. Have someone mark recommended four-step acceleration distances (listed below) on the court:

   • 26 to 30 inches between starting position and step 1,

   • 36 to 40 inches between step 1 and step 2,

   • 46 to 50 inches between step 2 and step 3, and

   • 56 to 60 inches between step 3 and step 4.

2. Start going through the four steps at quarter speed, avoiding any hesitation between the first and second step.

3. Make forceful moves—the more forceful you pump your arms, the more powerfully your opposite leg will drive.

4. Emphasize proper arm action and knee drive.

5. After you become proficient with the technique at quarter speed, you can gradu-ate to half effort, three-quarter effort, and then all-out effort.

After you learn to do the four-step exercise from a line, face the basket, turn, and start toward the other basket using the same four-step pattern. Other variations include changing from a backpedal to a sprint that emphasizes the first four steps or going from a defensive position into a sprint using the same idea.

Record of Speed

We've developed an easy-to-use chart (see chart 7-1) that you may copy from the book and use to keep a record of your speed work. Just place a check mark in the appropriate column on the chart as you complete each drill.

The drills in this chapter emphasized sprinting technique, but some of the same principles may apply to a variety of basketball movements, such as shuffling, backpedaling, defensive slides, and many other combinations. Apply the principles you have learned in this chapter with the sprinting program presented in chapter 3.

Proper mechanics and running form are essential for maximizing your speed. If you are patient in achieving the desired results and persistent in performing the recommended exercises, you'll be fast approaching your speed potential.

Chart 7-1
Speed Drill Chart

Exercise	Date	Date	Date	Date	Date	Date	Date	Date
Arm movement								
Running stride: A1								
A2								
A3								
B1								
B2								
B3								
C1								
C2								
Ankle flips								
Heel kicks								
4-Step acceleration								

AGILITY TRAINING

ecoming a top player takes more than practicing your jump shot. One of the best ways to raise your basketball performance to a higher level is to become a more well-rounded athlete. This is true whether you are trying to make your high school squad, earn a college scholarship, or reach the highest level of basketball—the NBA.

Every level of basketball competition demands the same athletic movements: sprint, change direction, get off the mark, turn and go, explode vertically once-twice-three times, speed up at various angles, and move from side to side with sudden bursts of speed in opposite directions. The combinations of these movements are countless because the players read and react to meet specific situations during each game. The great athletes in the NBA, like Gary Payton, Penny Hardaway, and Shawn Kemp, constantly create new movement combinations.

A player's ability to read and react in any given offensive or defensive situation is the essence of basketball intelligence. Your ability to apply a specific basketball skill is determined by your being able to move your body quickly and efficiently.

Agility refers to being able to change body direction quickly, explosively, efficiently, and in balance (under control). Players who can't make changes quickly struggle at both ends of the floor, especially when matched against more agile opponents. An unwritten rule in basketball states that for every level you go up in competition, your weakness will be magnified another degree.

For this reason alone, agility training must be an integral part of a basketball conditioning program. To get the job done, you must practice your basketball abilities both on and off the court. Just as a highly technical skill such as free-throw shooting requires hours of disciplined practice, so does the highly athletic skill of agility.

AGILITY TRIFECTA

Basketball demands dynamic, explosive, and repetitive movements. Therefore, agility involves the following qualities:

- Speed—the ability to move your body from one point to another running at 90 to 100 percent of your capacity
- Power—the ability to exert force in the shortest possible time
- Balance—the ability to regulate shifts in your body's center of gravity while maintaining control

Work on these three components of agility regularly to develop yourself as a basketball player. By performing leg-strengthening exercises (chapter 4), practicing plyometrics (chapter 6), and doing speed-training drills (chapter 7), you will greatly increase your agility.

The strength-training section will help you develop not only the legs but also the trunk area (lower back and abdominal muscles), which serves as a stabilizer to the lower extremities and allows for more independent and explosive movement through the leg and hip area. From the plyometrics section, emphasize lateral movements, changes of direction, and vertical jumps. As for the speed exercises, focus on starting ability, acceleration, stride frequency, and stride length. These exercises will make your movements more efficient and more agile.

LATERAL AGILITY

Basketball players must be able to move laterally quickly and smoothly. Lateral moves (step-drag or slide) initiate many changes in direction. Lateral movement requires that

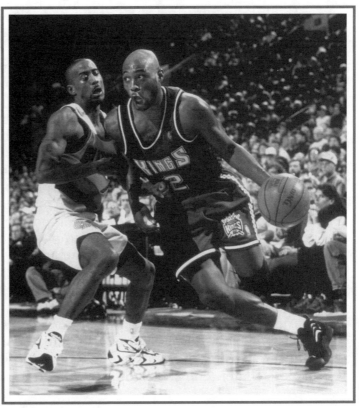

Agility training is an integral part of MItch Richmond's basketball conditioning program.

- your hips move, abduct and adduct, and flex and extend;
- your knee joints flex and extend; and
- your ankles dorsiflex and plantar-flex, and evert and invert.

Besides lateral moves, basketball players must be able to perform a variety of complex movements. Players must move through a number of horizontal planes (for example, sprint down the court) and vertical planes (for example, rise to shoot a jump shot) with agility.

Becoming agile in all these movements takes work. Just as strength-training exercises make your muscles stronger and plyometric exercises make your muscles more powerful, agility training will help you move more quickly and efficiently.

AGILITY-TRAINING TECHNIQUES

You should first master the technical form of basketball movements at slow speed. From there you can move to higher speeds. Never sacrifice technique for speed.

Essentially, you need to teach your feet what to do. The ground is required to produce force; you must plant your feet fully on the ground—not just push off with your toes. This is true whether you start from a static ready position or change direction at full speed.

Total foot contact with the ground's surface will produce the most power. Starting high on your toes is less powerful. Don't sit back on your heels either. Let your feet be in full contact with the ground. Your body weight should lean slightly forward onto the ball of each foot. This action permits you to push off powerfully with the balls of your feet.

Basketball requires players to make hundreds of unpredictable foot patterns during every game. When moving straight ahead, backward, or laterally, you must try to push the ground away from you. Spend as little time in the air as possible. This produces fewer vertical components in your stride.

To understand this technique, watch another player's head. If it stays level, his or her form is fine; if you notice any bobbing action, it isn't.

Keep your knees flexed and situated over your toes, but never extend them fully. Your hips will move and, more important, will not settle too close to the ground when you come to a full stop or change direction. Let your trunk remain tall and sit just over your hips.

Do this without any excess forward or backward leaning or rocking. This ensures that your body's center of gravity will remain in the most efficient position possible while producing the most efficient movement possible.

Each sport requires unique movement patterns. Fortunately, you can rehearse many of these before competition. For instance, a tennis player can rehearse moving to the forehand side, hitting the ball, and then recovering back to center. The shortstop can rehearse going into the deep hole in either

Gary Payton performs a lateral agility drill with strength and conditioning coach Bob Medina timing him.

direction. The volleyball player can rehearse advancing to the net and then backing off.

Many of these movements have a natural rhythm that you can rehearse hundreds of times before competition. Try practicing your movements in slow motion. This gives you enough time to work on improving your technique, balance, coordination, and concentration.

An effective agility-training program includes drills that

- are short in duration (anaerobic);
- require at least two or three directional changes;
- focus on lateral movement;
- mix lateral with straight-ahead and backpedaling movements, thereby producing quick rotations;
- include countermoves going in the opposite direction; and
- demand ankle agility.

TRAINING SCHEDULE

You'll get greatest results in agility conditioning during the off-season and preseason periods. During these times you can work at your highest intensity and still allow for sufficient recovery time. The results from this work will carry over into the regular season, and you should be able to maintain your off-season progress through the entire season. If you play a lot of minutes in games and get plenty of practice time, it will be easy to maintain your high level of conditioning. If you receive limited playing time, you must put in extra work before or after practice to maintain your progress. During the off-season, we recommend performing agility drills twice a week, on Monday and Thursday (see complete power conditioning program in chapter 10).

AGILITY DRILLS

You can do the following drills individually or as a team. To ensure that your technique is correct, perform the drills under the watchful eye of a coach or have someone videotape your workout and then review it with your coach.

Agility drill work is important throughout the year but especially during the off-season and preseason. In-season, you can devote less time to agility work because games and practices will require the use of the same agility skills you developed in the off-season. Also, intensity levels are highest during games and practices.

Most of the drills take no longer than 10 seconds and are predominantly anaerobic. You should perform the drills at maximum speed and intensity for best development. Be sure that in all your drills you focus on quality execution rather than just going through the motions. If fatigue sets in, stop the drill until you have adequately recovered for the next bout.

COMPLETE THE SQUARE

1. Start in a ready position at the corner of the left side of the baseline.

2. Make four consecutive trips around the lane—two clockwise (trips 1 and 3) and two counterclockwise (trips 2 and 4).

3. On "Go," sprint forward down the lane. Upon reaching the free-throw line, slide to the right until you reach the opposite lane line. Backpedal down the lane to the right edge of the baseline and then slide left back to the starting position.

4. When you reach the starting point, repeat the drill going in the opposite direction.

5. Continue the drill until you've completed two clockwise trips and two counterclockwise trips. Four total trips around the lane count as one drill.

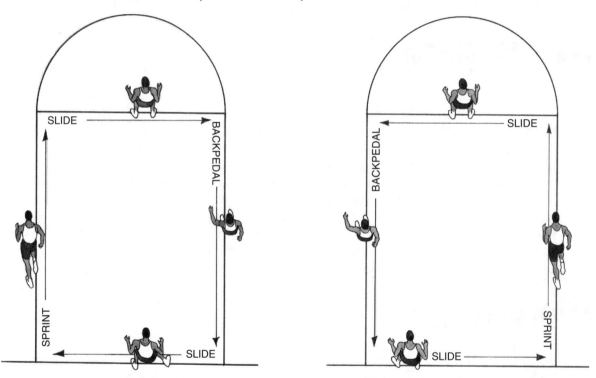

COMPLETE THE SQUARE (WITH ROPE)

1. Start in a ready jump-rope position at the corner of the left side of the free-throw line.

2. Make two consecutive trips around the lane—one clockwise (trip 1) and one counterclockwise (trip 2).

   • Forward: Work down the lane, moving forward in any number of foot patterns of choice with the jump rope.

     - Soft pitter-pat run

     - Double-leg soft hop

- Single-leg soft hop

- Single-leg soft hop at 45-degree angles

- Side: Upon reaching the edge of the baseline and lane, work to the right again, using any of the following foot patterns:

  - Double-leg soft hop to the right

  - Single-leg (right or left) soft hop

  - High-knees working to the right

- Back: Upon reaching the opposite edge of the lane, work backward up the lane, using any of the following patterns:

  - Soft backpedal

  - Double-leg soft hop backward

  - High-knees backward

- Side: At the right edge of the foul line, work on any of the side movements already listed earlier, moving back to start. When you reach the start, reverse direction (counterclockwise) and do the pattern of your choice. Your goal for the two trips is to complete both trips without stopping.

STAR RUNS IN THE LANE

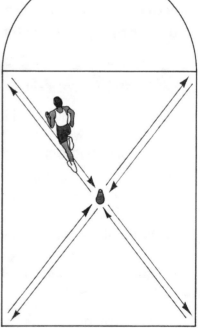

1. Place a marker (tape or cone) in the center of the foul lane.

2. Start in a ready position, then race to any corner of the lane.

3. Race back to the center, then move to a corner of your choice until you complete all four corners.

4. Do two repetitions each of the following five foot patterns:

   - Sprint forward to corner and sprint back to center.

   - Backpedal to corner and sprint forward to center.

   - Slide laterally to corner and slide back to center.

   - Slide to corner and sprint back to center.

   - Sprint to corner and slide back to center.

RICOCHET PICK-UPS

1. Stand in ready position three to five yards from a wall with the ball in both hands, feet spread slightly wider than normal. Hold ball low, close to floor.

2. Bounce the ball low off the wall at an angle and slide laterally to retrieve it, never crossing your feet. You must play the ball low (one to one and a half feet) off the wall so that it rolls back. Don't chest pass the ball off the wall; try to throw it underhand, using two hands to catch and pass.

3. Catch the ball, then bounce it off the wall to the other side, slide, and retrieve it.

4. Continue to work side to side.

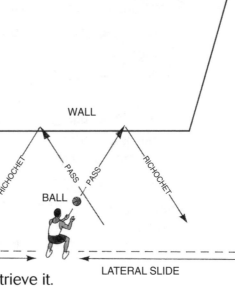

Duration: 10 to 15 seconds

Changes of direction during drill: four to six

Intensity: low to maximum (depending on phase)

Recovery time: 30 to 60 seconds (depending on intensity)

Number of repetitions: 6 to 12 (depending on phase)

LATERAL SLIDE WITH RESPONSE

1. Stand in a ready position at the free-throw line with a coach or partner standing behind you.

2. On "Go," slide right (laterally) toward the sideline without crossing your feet.

3. When the coach or partner claps, change direction quickly and slide toward the other sideline.

   Keep changing directions whenever you hear a clap.

Note: You can perform this drill with one player or a full team. If done with a full team, split the team into two groups; one half works while the other rests.

Duration: 8 to 10 seconds

Changes of direction during drill: four to six

Intensity: low to maximum (depending on phase)

Recovery time: 30 to 60 seconds (depending on intensity)

Number of repetitions: 6 to 12 (depending on phase)

THE WHEEL

1. Pair up a larger and smaller player (six pairs). If you have fewer players, you can use cones.
2. Have the players form a circle 7 to 10 yards in diameter, equidistant from the center jump circle.
3. Have smaller players walk to center with larger players staying in place and serving as outside markers.

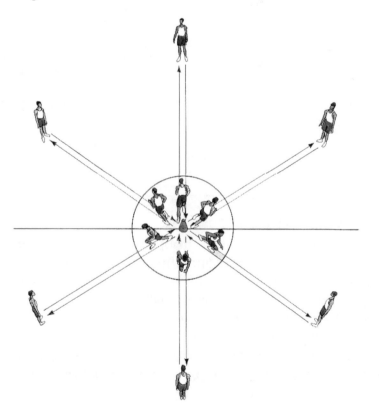

4. On "Go," all the smaller players sprint to their partners first, touch hand of partner, then sprint back to center. After completion of the first run they will continue in a clockwise fashion, touching all six outside markers, always returning to the center after they touch each outside marker. All smaller players run at same time, and the drill is complete when all of them finish in center circle.
5. Smaller players now replace the larger players as markers on outside, and larger players perform drill.

Variations:

- Face into center circle and backpedal to and around partner, then sprint back to center.
- Perform defensive slides around marker, then sprint back to center.

GASSER ROTATIONS

1. Break team into three groups of equal speed ability.
2. Line one group along one free-throw line. Line the other two groups at the opposite foul line with one group behind the other group.
3. Place three or four cones in a straight line about two to two and a half yards from the foul line, then string out cones.

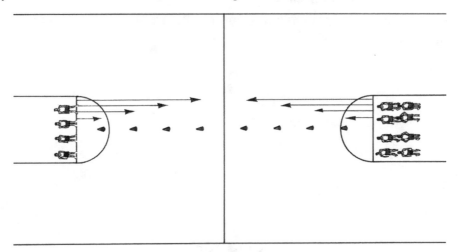

4. Foul lines serve as starting positions.
5. Drill begins with the first of two groups at one end sprinting to first cone, racing back to the foul line, then sprinting to second cone and back to foul line until all the cones at one end have been used. After completion of cone drill, this group will sprint to the resting group at the opposite foul line. Once the working group passes the foul line, the next group will perform the same drill at the other end. Upon completion they will then sprint to the final group, who perform the same drill to complete the rotation. Groups will do 6 to 10 rotations. This gives a 1:2 work-to-rest ratio during the drill.

Variations:

- Sprint to cone, turn, and sprint back to foul line.
- Sprint to cone and backpedal to foul line.
- Sprint to cone and perform defensive 45-degree slides to foul line.
- Perform lateral slide to cone and lateral slide back to foul line.
- Perform lateral slide to cone and sprint back to foul line.
- Sprint to cone and perform lateral slide to foul line.

PART

IV

Power Rating and Programming

BASKETBALL CONDITIONING POWER RATING SYSTEM

e've covered all the components to power conditioning for basketball. But those concepts are useful only if we have a way to measure them. That's why we developed the Basketball Conditioning (BC) Power Rating System.

This system is a series of self-tests on these key conditioning components: power, agility, conditioning, muscle strength and endurance, flexibility, and percentage of body fat. Strive toward the goal of achieving a perfect score (10) on each of the tests, then work to maintain that high level of conditioning. As you improve in each conditioning category, you'll become a better athlete and a better basketball player.

Before attempting these tests, be sure to warm up and stretch out as instructed in chapter 1. We've designed the power rating for your individual development, which should be your first concern. As you become more familiar with the tests and develop physically, you can use the system to monitor your improvements and have some fun competing against your teammates.

POWER: VERTICAL JUMP

The vertical jump test is a good measure of the explosive power of the lower body. The test is done in two phases: the standing reach and the jump reach. Your vertical jump is the difference between the two measures.

Standing Reach

1. Stand sideways next to a wall with your feet flat on the floor.
2. Mark the fingertips of your reaching hand with chalk.
3. Reach with that arm as high as possible and make a chalk mark on the wall.
4. Tape a yardstick to the wall, with the bottom of the stick resting on the chalk mark and the top of the stick pointing toward the ceiling.

Jump Reach

1. Rechalk your fingertips.
2. Stand sideways next to the wall and jump as high as possible, tapping the yardstick with your fingertips. (Don't take a step before jumping.)
3. Jump three times and record your best height.

Juwan Howard shows his vertical jump while shooting during competition.

Table 9-1
Vertical Jump Power Rating
Height (in inches)

Females	Males	Rating
≥21	≥34	10
20	32	9
19	30	8
18	28	7
17	26	6
16	24	5
15	22	4
14	20	3
13	18	2
≤12	≤16	1

4. The difference between the standing reach and the jump reach is your vertical jump.

See table 9-1 for ratings and use chart 9-1 to record your progress.

Chart 9-1
Vertical Jump
(to be filled in monthly)

Date	Score	Rating	Date	Score	Rating

AGILITY: 20-YARD DRILL

The 20-yard agility drill measures your ability to accelerate, decelerate, and change direction. Here's how to do it.

1. On a flat surface (preferably a gym or possibly a driveway), place a two-foot piece of tape to mark a center line. Measure five yards in both directions from the center line and mark these spots with the tape.

2. Have a coach or partner time you.

3. Straddle the center line with your feet an equal distance from the line and place one hand on the line.

4. On the command "Ready Go," run toward the line of your choice and touch it with your hand and foot.

5. Change direction and run past the center line to the opposite line and touch it with your hand and foot.

Table 9-2 20-Yard Agility Power Rating Time (in seconds)		
Females	Males	Rating
≤4.5	≤4.0	10
4.8	4.3	9
5.1	4.6	8
5.4	4.9	7
5.7	5.2	6
6.0	5.5	5
6.3	5.8	4
6.6	6.1	3
6.9	6.4	2
≥7.2	≥6.7	1

6. Again, change direction and run through the center line. This time do not touch the center line with your hand and foot.

7. The drill is over when you cross the center line the second time. Record the best of three trials.

See table 9-2 for ratings and use chart 9-2 to record your progress.

Chart 9-2 20-Yard Agility Drill (to be filled in monthly)					
Date	Score	Rating	Date	Score	Rating

CONDITIONING: 300-YARD SHUTTLE

The 300-yard shuttle measures anaerobic endurance. Here's the test:

1. On a flat surface (preferably a gym or track), measure and mark 25 yards.
2. Run to the 25-yard mark, touch it with your foot, then turn and run back to the start. Repeat this six times without stopping.
3. Rest five minutes and repeat the shuttle.
4. Record the average of the two times.

See table 9-3 for ratings and use chart 9-3 to record your progress.

Table 9-3
300-Yard Shuttle Power Rating
Time (in seconds)

Females	Males	Rating
≤50.9	≤45.9	10
51-52.9	46-47.9	9
53-54.9	48-49.9	8
55-56.9	50-51.9	7
57-58.9	52-53.9	6
59-60.9	54-55.9	5
61-62.9	56-57.9	4
63-64.9	58-59.9	3
65-66.9	60-61.9	2
≥67.0	≥62.0	1

Chart 9-3
300-Yard Shuttle
(to be filled in monthly)

Date	Score	Rating	Date	Score	Rating

MUSCLE STRENGTH AND ENDURANCE: PUSH-UPS, PULL-UPS, AND SIT-UPS

The push-up, pull-up, and sit-up tests measure muscular strength and endurance in the upper body and torso.

Push-Ups

1. Assume a proper push-up starting position: straight arms with hands flat on the floor, your thumbs directly below your armpits, and your fingers pointing forward. Your shoulders, back, buttocks, and legs are in a flat, straight position with toes touching the floor.
2. Place a rolled towel (two inches high) on the floor directly below your chest.
3. Lower your body under control until your chest touches the towel and then push your body up until your arms are fully extended.
4. Count the total number of completed reps. Don't count a rep unless you touch the towel, your body stayed in straight alignment throughout the movement, and your arms are fully extended.
5. The test is over when you can't do a complete push-up.

See table 9-4 for ratings and use chart 9-4 to record your progress.

Table 9-4
Push-Ups Power Rating
Number of Push-Ups

Females	Males	Rating
≥30	≥60	10
27-29	55-59	9
24-26	50-54	8
21-23	45-49	7
18-20	40-44	6
15-17	35-39	5
12-14	30-34	4
9-11	25-29	3
6-8	20-24	2
≤5	≤19	1

	Chart 9-4				
	Push-Ups				
	(to be filled in monthly)				
Date	Score	Rating	Date	Score	Rating

Pull-Ups

1. Position your hands on the bar with palms facing away, shoulder-width apart, and arms in a fully extended hanging position. The pull-up bar should be high enough to allow you to hang in a fully extended position without having your feet touching the floor.

2. Pull yourself up until your chin is above the bar and return to a fully extended hanging position.

3. Count the total number of completed repetitions. Don't count reps if (a) your chin doesn't clear the bar, (b) your arms fail to fully extend, or (c) your body swings.

4. The test is over when you fail to complete the upward movement or you don't begin the upward movement within five seconds of completing a repetition.

See table 9-5 for ratings and use chart 9-5 to record your progress.

Table 9-5
Pull-Ups Power Rating
Number of Pull-Ups

Females	Males	Rating
≥9	≥16	10
8	14-15	9
7	12-13	8
6	10-11	7
5	8-9	6
4	6-7	5
3	4-5	4
2	3	3
1	2	2
0	≤1	1

Chart 9-5
Pull-Ups
(to be filled in monthly)

Date	Score	Rating	Date	Score	Rating

Sit-Ups

1. Lie on the floor with your knees bent so that your heels are 12 to 18 inches from your buttocks. Place your hands behind your head and interlock your fingers.

2. Your partner will hold your feet in position, count your repetitions, and time you for 60 seconds.

3. On command, sit up until your elbows touch your knees, and lie back until your shoulder blades touch the floor. Repeat as many times as possible for 60 seconds. Don't count reps if (a) your elbows don't touch your knees, (b) your shoulder blades don't touch the floor, or (c) your fingers and hands separate, or your hands come over the top of your head.

Table 9-6 Sit-Ups Power Rating Number of Sit-Ups		
Females	**Males**	**Rating**
≥55	≥60	10
50-54	55-59	9
45-49	50-54	8
40-44	45-49	7
35-39	40-44	6
30-34	35-39	5
25-29	30-34	4
20-24	25-29	3
15-19	20-24	2
≤14	≤19	1

See table 9-6 for ratings and use chart 9-6 to record your progress.

Chart 9-6 Sit-Ups (to be filled in monthly)					
Date	**Score**	**Rating**	**Date**	**Score**	**Rating**

FLEXIBILITY: SIT-AND-REACH

The sit-and-reach test measures hamstring and low-back flexibility. Here's how to do it.

1. Sit with your legs extended in front of you and the bottom of your feet touching the bottom step of a flight of stairs; your feet should be about six inches apart.

2. Set a ruler on the first step so it overhangs in your direction. The inch mark on the ruler that marks the bottom of your feet will be zero for the test. Reaching beyond your feet indicates positive numbers. Not reaching your feet are negative numbers.

3. Keeping your legs straight, bend forward slowly from the waist with your arms outstretched, your hands together, and your palms down.

4. Reach as far as you can with your hands at toe level. Hold for two seconds, repeat three times, and record your best score.

See table 9-7 for ratings and use chart 9-7 to record your progress.

Table 9-7
Sit-and-Reach Power Rating
Measured in inches

Females	Males	Rating
≥12	≥10	10
+10	+8	9
+8	+6	8
+6	+4	7
+4	+2	6
+2	0	5
0	–2	4
–2	–4	3
–4	–6	2
≤–6	≤–8	1

Chart 9-7 Sit-and-Reach (to be filled in monthly)					
Date	**Score**	**Rating**	**Date**	**Score**	**Rating**

BODY COMPOSITION: SKINFOLD TEST

The percentage of fat in the body is a critical measure of overall fitness. Hauling extra pounds of fat up and down the floor will fatigue a player quickly. Most NBA players have less than 10 percent body fat, confirming that they are lean and well-muscled athletes.

The most effective way to check your body fat is by underwater weighing. It's an expensive procedure and requires elaborate equipment and trained staff, so we'll present a more realistic option.

Perhaps the easiest way to determine body composition is to use a skinfold caliper. Consult an athletic trainer, conditioning coach, physical education teacher, or other trained professional to get your body-fat percentage measurement.

The skinfold test involves pinching the skin at three to seven sites on the body and measuring the thickness of each fold with the caliper. The measurements you obtain at each site are totaled and then referenced to a standardized chart for the appropriate age and sex. Acceptable ranges for basketball players are 6 to 14 percent for males and 12 to 20 percent for females.

See table 9-8 for ratings and use chart 9-8 to record your progress.

Table 9-8
Body Composition Rating
Percentage of body fat

Females	Males	Rating
12.0-13.5	6-7.5	10
13.6-15	7.6-9	9
15.1-16.5	9.1-10.5	8
16.6-18	10.6-12	7
18.1-19.5	12.1-13.5	6
19.6-21	13.6-15	5
21.1-22.5	15.1-16.5	4
22.6-24	16.6-18	3
24.1-25.5	18.1-19.5	2
≥25.6	≥19.6	1

Chart 9-8
Body Composition
(to be filled in monthly)

Date	Score	Rating	Date	Score	Rating

BC POWER RATING

Perform the tests in this chapter and fill out the BC Power Rating chart (see chart 9-9) once a month. With effective conditioning, you'll notice steady progress within 6 to 12 months. Work hard, and don't become discouraged. You can do it!

BC POWER RATING AGE-GROUP AVERAGES

Junior High School (12 to 14 years old)	2 to 4
High School (15 to 17 years old)	4 to 6
College (18 to 21 years old)	6 to 8

Chart 9-9
BC Power Rating

Test	Date Score/Rating	Date Score/Rating	Date Score/Rating	Date Score/Rating	Date Score/Rating	Date Score/Rating	Date Score/Rating	Date Score/Rating	Date Score/Rating
Vertical jump (inches)									
20-Yard agility (seconds)									
300-Yard shuttle (seconds)									
Push-ups (repetitions)									
Pull-ups (repetitions)									
Sit-ups (repetitions)									
Sit-and-reach (inches)									
Body composition (percentages)									
Total									
Divide by 8									
BC Power Rating									

COMPLETE POWER
CONDITIONING PROGRAM

ach area discussed in this book will help you to be a better athlete. But to become the best athlete you can be, you must have a well rounded program that includes all the areas covered in this book.

The stretching, warm-up, and cool-down program will help to reduce injuries and improve performance. The power nutrition plan will give you the energy you will need to train at high levels of intensity to become a better athlete. The conditioning program will improve your anaerobic endurance and improve your overall conditioning tremendously. The strength training program will develop a solid total body strength base which will help to reduce injuries and improve performance. The plyometric training program will improve your explosive power so you will jump higher and run faster. The agility training program will improve your quickness and your ability to change directions.

If you just do some parts of the complete power conditioning program and neglect other areas, your improvement may be minimal. Remember, becoming a well rounded athlete involves each of these components.

Some highly motivated young athletes will want to do more than what we recommend on a daily basis. This may lead to overtraining and a decrease in performance. For best results, follow the program as outlined.

The calendar on the following pages shows you how the complete program fits together. This calendar shows a 12-week complete program. When you begin the program, the exercises are intended to be low-intensity, high-volume. The low-intensity, high-volume phase should be followed by higher intensity, lower volume, with peaking at the end of the program. The calendar is intended for you to use as a daily check system to monitor your complete program.

HOW THE PROGRAM WORKS

The boxes for Monday and Thursday on the next page show that workouts start with a warm-up and stretch. That is followed by the upper-body weight-training program, the plyometric training, and the agility drills. The workout is finished after a good cool-down. You can do the plyometrics and agilities before the upper-body weight training.

Like all workouts, Tuesday and Friday workouts begin with a warm-up and stretching (see the boxes on the next page). This is followed by the lower-body weight-training program. During the first six weeks of the program, the strides are done after the lower body weight training. When the sprinting program starts during week 7, you have two choices: You can do your sprints before your lower body weight training or you can do your sprints on Wednesdays and Saturdays. Again, you should finish your workouts with a cool-down.

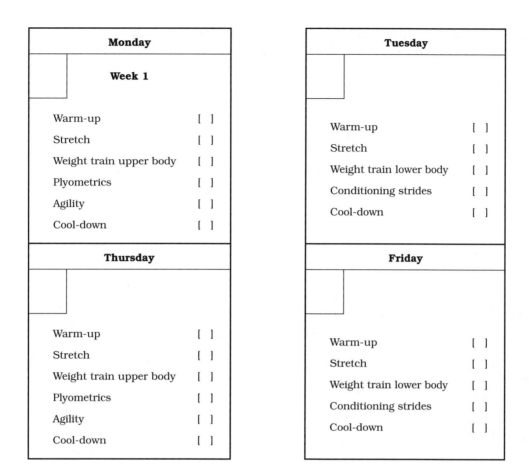

Monday	
Week 1	
Warm-up	[ ]
Stretch	[ ]
Weight train upper body	[ ]
Plyometrics	[ ]
Agility	[ ]
Cool-down	[ ]

Tuesday	
Warm-up	[ ]
Stretch	[ ]
Weight train lower body	[ ]
Conditioning strides	[ ]
Cool-down	[ ]

Thursday	
Warm-up	[ ]
Stretch	[ ]
Weight train upper body	[ ]
Plyometrics	[ ]
Agility	[ ]
Cool-down	[ ]

Friday	
Warm-up	[ ]
Stretch	[ ]
Weight train lower body	[ ]
Conditioning strides	[ ]
Cool-down	[ ]

The speed drills are not listed on the twelve week calendar. These drills can be used on Wednesdays and Saturdays starting week 7.

SAMPLE PROGRAM

Following is a sample 12-week complete program.

Chart 10-1
Off-Season Total Program

Month _____ Year _____

	Monday	Tuesday	Wednesday	Thursday	Friday	Saturday
Week 1	Warm-up [ ] Stretch [ ] Weight train upper body [ ] Plyometrics [ ] Agility [ ] Cool-down [ ]	Warm-up [ ] Stretch [ ] Weight train lower body [ ] Conditioning strides [ ] Cool-down [ ]		Warm-up [ ] Stretch [ ] Weight train upper body [ ] Plyometrics [ ] Agility [ ] Cool-down [ ]	Warm-up [ ] Stretch [ ] Weight train lower body [ ] Conditioning strides [ ] Cool-down [ ]	
Week 2	Warm-up [ ] Stretch [ ] Weight train upper body [ ] Plyometrics [ ] Agility [ ] Cool-down [ ]	Warm-up [ ] Stretch [ ] Weight train lower body [ ] Conditioning strides [ ] Cool-down [ ]		Warm-up [ ] Stretch [ ] Weight train upper body [ ] Plyometrics [ ] Agility [ ] Cool-down [ ]	Warm-up [ ] Stretch [ ] Weight train lower body [ ] Conditioning strides [ ] Cool-down [ ]	
Week 3	Warm-up [ ] Stretch [ ] Weight train upper body [ ] Plyometrics [ ] Agility [ ] Cool-down [ ]	Warm-up [ ] Stretch [ ] Weight train lower body [ ] Conditioning strides [ ] Cool-down [ ]		Warm-up [ ] Stretch [ ] Weight train upper body [ ] Plyometrics [ ] Agility [ ] Cool-down [ ]	Warm-up [ ] Stretch [ ] Weight train lower body [ ] Conditioning strides [ ] Cool-down [ ]	
Week 4	Warm-up [ ] Stretch [ ] Weight train upper body [ ] Plyometrics [ ] Agility [ ] Cool-down [ ]	Warm-up [ ] Stretch [ ] Weight train lower body [ ] Conditioning strides [ ] Cool-down [ ]		Warm-up [ ] Stretch [ ] Weight train upper body [ ] Plyometrics [ ] Agility [ ] Cool-down [ ]	Warm-up [ ] Stretch [ ] Weight train lower body [ ] Conditioning strides [ ] Cool-down [ ]	

Chart 10-1
Off-Season Total Program (continued)

Month _____   Year _____

Monday	Tuesday	Wednesday	Thursday	Friday	Saturday
Week 5					
Warm-up [ ] Stretch [ ] Weight train upper body [ ] Plyometrics [ ] Agility [ ] Cool-down [ ]	Warm-up [ ] Stretch [ ] Weight train lower body [ ] Conditioning strides [ ] Cool-down [ ]		Warm-up [ ] Stretch [ ] Weight train upper body [ ] Plyometrics [ ] Agility [ ] Cool-down [ ]	Warm-up [ ] Stretch [ ] Weight train lower body [ ] Conditioning strides [ ] Cool-down [ ]	
Week 6					
Warm-up [ ] Stretch [ ] Weight train upper body [ ] Plyometrics [ ] Agility [ ] Cool-down [ ]	Warm-up [ ] Stretch [ ] Weight train lower body [ ] Conditioning strides [ ] Cool-down [ ]		Warm-up [ ] Stretch [ ] Weight train upper body [ ] Plyometrics [ ] Agility [ ] Cool-down [ ]	Warm-up [ ] Stretch [ ] Weight train lower body [ ] Conditioning strides [ ] Cool-down [ ]	
Week 7					
Warm-up [ ] Stretch [ ] Weight train upper body [ ] Plyometrics [ ] Agility [ ] Cool-down [ ]	Warm-up [ ] Stretch [ ] Weight train lower body [ ] Conditioning sprints* [ ] Cool-down [ ]	Sprints* [ ]	Warm-up [ ] Stretch [ ] Weight train upper body [ ] Plyometrics [ ] Agility [ ] Cool-down [ ]	Warm-up [ ] Stretch [ ] Weight train lower body [ ] Conditioning sprints* [ ] Cool-down [ ]	Sprints* [ ]
Week 8					
Warm-up [ ] Stretch [ ] Weight train upper body [ ] Plyometrics [ ] Agility [ ] Cool-down [ ]	Warm-up [ ] Stretch [ ] Weight train lower body [ ] Conditioning sprints* [ ] Cool-down [ ]	Sprints* [ ]	Warm-up [ ] Stretch [ ] Weight train upper body [ ] Plyometrics [ ] Agility [ ] Cool-down [ ]	Warm-up [ ] Stretch [ ] Weight train lower body [ ] Conditioning sprints* [ ] Cool-down [ ]	Sprints* [ ]

*If you do the sprints on Tuesdays and Fridays, they need to be done before weight training.

(continued)

Chart 10-1
Off-Season Total Program (continued)

Month _____ Year _____

	Monday	Tuesday	Wednesday	Thursday	Friday	Saturday
Week 9	Warm-up [ ] Stretch [ ] Weight train upper body [ ] Plyometrics [ ] Agility [ ] Cool-down [ ]	Warm-up [ ] Stretch [ ] Weight train lower body [ ] Conditioning sprints* [ ] Cool-down [ ]	Sprints* [ ]	Warm-up [ ] Stretch [ ] Weight train upper body [ ] Plyometrics [ ] Agility [ ] Cool-down [ ]	Warm-up [ ] Stretch [ ] Weight train lower body [ ] Conditioning sprints* [ ] Cool-down [ ]	Sprints* [ ]
Week 10	Warm-up [ ] Stretch [ ] Weight train upper body [ ] Plyometrics [ ] Agility [ ] Cool-down [ ]	Warm-up [ ] Stretch [ ] Weight train lower body [ ] Conditioning sprints* [ ] Cool-down [ ]	Sprints* [ ]	Warm-up [ ] Stretch [ ] Weight train upper body [ ] Plyometrics [ ] Agility [ ] Cool-down [ ]	Warm-up [ ] Stretch [ ] Weight train lower body [ ] Conditioning sprints* [ ] Cool-down [ ]	Sprints* [ ]
Week 11	Warm-up [ ] Stretch [ ] Weight train upper body [ ] Plyometrics [ ] Agility [ ] Cool-down [ ]	Warm-up [ ] Stretch [ ] Weight train lower body [ ] Conditioning sprints* [ ] Cool-down [ ]	Sprints* [ ]	Warm-up [ ] Stretch [ ] Weight train upper body [ ] Plyometrics [ ] Agility [ ] Cool-down [ ]	Warm-up [ ] Stretch [ ] Weight train lower body [ ] Conditioning sprints* [ ] Cool-down [ ]	Sprints* [ ]
Week 12	Warm-up [ ] Stretch [ ] Weight train upper body [ ] Plyometrics [ ] Agility [ ] Cool-down [ ]	Warm-up [ ] Stretch [ ] Weight train lower body [ ] Conditioning sprints* [ ] Cool-down [ ]	Sprints* [ ]	Warm-up [ ] Stretch [ ] Weight train upper body [ ] Plyometrics [ ] Agility [ ] Cool-down [ ]	Warm-up [ ] Stretch [ ] Weight train lower body [ ] Conditioning sprints* [ ] Cool-down [ ]	Sprints* [ ]

*If you do the sprints on Tuesdays and Fridays, they need to be done before weight training.

APPENDIX

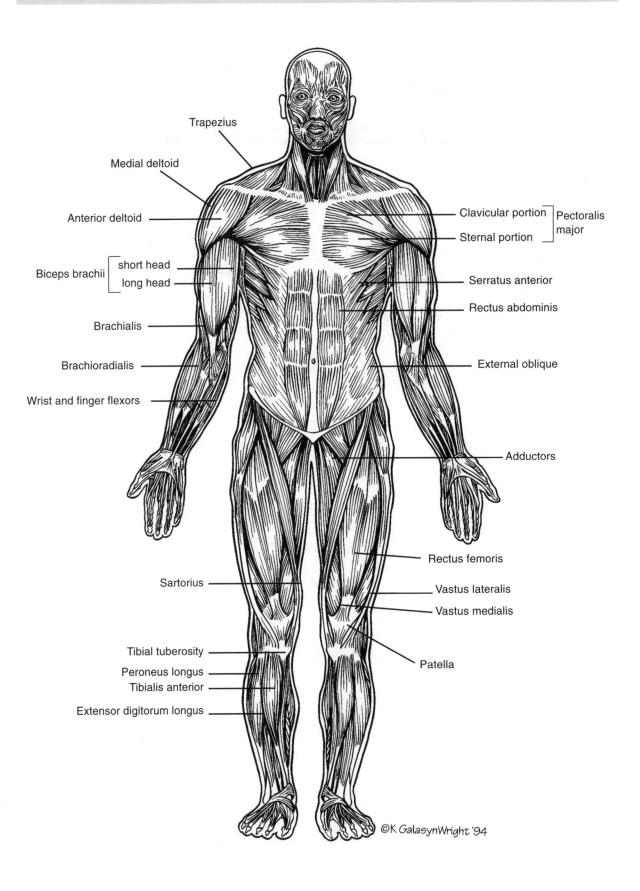

Trapezius

Medial deltoid

Anterior deltoid

Biceps brachii { short head
                 long head

Brachialis

Brachioradialis

Wrist and finger flexors

Sartorius

Tibial tuberosity

Peroneus longus

Tibialis anterior

Extensor digitorum longus

Clavicular portion] Pectoralis
Sternal portion   ] major

Serratus anterior

Rectus abdominis

External oblique

Adductors

Rectus femoris

Vastus lateralis

Vastus medialis

Patella

©K GalasynWright '94

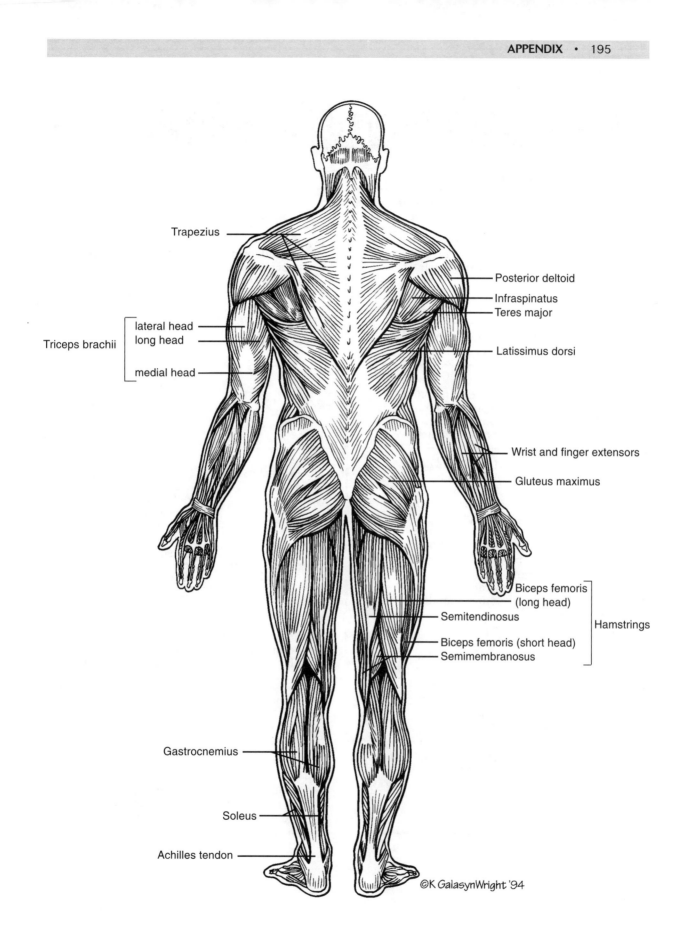

Trapezius

Posterior deltoid

Infraspinatus

Teres major

Triceps brachii
- lateral head
- long head
- medial head

Latissimus dorsi

Wrist and finger extensors

Gluteus maximus

Biceps femoris (long head)

Semitendinosus

Biceps femoris (short head)

Semimembranosus

Hamstrings

Gastrocnemius

Soleus

Achilles tendon

©K GalasynWright '94

Table A-1
Major Muscles Worked in Exercises

UPPER BODY		LOWER BODY & MIDSECTION	
Exercises	**Major Muscles Worked**	**Exercises**	**Major Muscles Worked**

Bench press
Incline press
Bar dips
	Pectoralis major
	Anterior deltoid
	Triceps brachii
		Leg raises
		Sit-ups (all forms)
		Crunches involve
		  no hip flexors
			Rectus abdominis
			Obliques (internal
			  and external)
			Hip flexors
			  1. iliopsoas
			  2. rectus femoris

Lat pull-downs
Pull-ups
	Latissimus dorsi
	Rhomboids
	Teres major
	Brachioradialis
	Biceps brachii
		Straight leg dead lifts
		Back extensions
			Gluteals
			Erector spinae
			  1. spinalis
			  2. longissimus
			  3. iliocostalis
			Hamstrings
			  1. biceps femoris
			  2. semimembranosus
			  3. semitendinosus

Military press Push press	Deltoids Triceps brachii Upper trapezius Supraspinatus Serratus anterior		

Seated lat row
Dumbbell lat row
	Latissimus dorsi
	Rhomboids
	Teres major
	Posterior deltoid
	Biceps brachii
	Brachioradialis
	Erector spinae
		Squats
		Leg press/hip sled
		Lunges
		Step-ups
			Quadriceps femoris
			  1. rectus femoris
			  2. vastus medialis
			  3. vastus intermedius
			  4. vastus lateralis
			Gluteals
			Erector spinae
			  (squats only)

Lateral dumbbell raise	Deltoids Trapezius Supraspinatus	Leg extensions	Quadriceps femoris
		Leg curls: standing or lying	Hamstrings

Upright rows	Trapezius
	Deltoids
	Biceps brachii
	Levator scapulae
	Brachioradialis
		Abductor machine
		  (lateral hip),
		  pulley or lying
			Abductors
			  1. tensor fasciae latae
			  2. gluteus medius
			  3. gluteus minimus

Tricep extensions
Tricep pressdowns
	Triceps brachii
	Anconeus
		Adductor machine
		  (inner thigh),
		  pulley or lying
		Side lunges
			Adductors
			  1. pectineus
			  2. gracilis
			  3. adductor brevis
			  4. adductor longus
			  5. adductor magnus

Bicep curls	Biceps brachii
	Brachialis
		Standing heel raises
		Seated heel raises
			Calves
			  1. gastrocnemius
			  2. soleus

Table A-2
Fastbreak Food Chart
Samples of foods and their approximate nutritional makeup in grams

	Calories	Protein	Carbohydrates	Fat
Fruits				
Apple, 1 medium	86	0	21	0.2
Banana, 1 medium	114	1	27	0.2
Orange, 1 medium	64	1	15	0.0
Grapes, 1/2 cup	38	0	9	0.2
Peach, 1 medium	44	1	10	0.0
Cantaloupe, 1/4 medium	32	1	7	0.0
Pear, 1 medium	104	1	25	0.0
Strawberry, 1/2 cup	28	1	6	0.0
Pineapple, 1 large slice	96	0	24	0.0
Grains				
White bread, 1 slice	65	2	12	1
Wheat bread, 1 slice	65	2	12	1
Spaghetti, 1 cup	157	5	32	1
Bagel	154	6	28	2
Corn flakes, 3/4 cup	70	2	16	0
Graham crackers, 2	53	1	10	1
Oatmeal, 1/2 cup	65	2	12	1
Vegetables				
Green beans, 1 cup	30	1.6	5.4	0.2
Corn, 1 cup	157	5.0	34	0.1
Carrots, 1	33	1.0	7	0.1
Baked potato, plain	225	5.0	51	0.1
Tomato, 1/2 medium	24	1.0	5	0.0
Broccoli, 1 cup	56	5.0	9	0.0
Meat				
Chicken (roasted), 1/2 breast	135	27	0	3
Sausage, 1 link	170	2	0	18
Ground beef (broiled), 3 oz	242	20	0	18
Tuna, 2.5 oz	124	30	1	0
Ham (baked), 2 slices	94	10	0	6
Dairy				
Milk (whole), 1 cup	148	8	11	8
Milk (2%), 1 cup	125	8	12	5
Milk (skim), 1 cup	80	8	12	0
Mozzarella cheese, 1 oz	82	6	1	6
Swiss cheese, 1 oz	108	8	1	8
Cream cheese, 1 oz	102	2	1	10
Butter, 1 tbsp	99	0	0	11
Margarine, 1 tbsp	99	0	0	11
Ice cream, 1 cup	274	5	32	14
Frozen yogurt, 1 cup	119	3	20	3

FOOD RECORD CHART

After reading the nutrition chapter (chapter 2), you may be curious about how many calories and grams of carbohydrates, protein, and fat you eat in a day. You can chart this information on the food record chart. If you need more information, there are many books, including *Nancy Clark's Sports Nutrition Guidebook*, that offer complete nutritional make-up of common foods.

Chart A-1 Food Record Chart				
Food	**Protein** (4 calories per gram)	**Carbohydrates** (4 calories per gram)	**Fat** (9 calories per gram)	**Calories**

GLOSSARY

agonist (prime mover)—Muscle primarily responsible for performing a movement.

antagonist—Muscle or group of muscles that are opposing the prime mover muscle or muscle group.

body building—Sport in which the body is judged according to various posing positions displaying muscular development, size, balance, and definition.

circuit training—Type of resistance training that is time controlled with a specific exercise order. The work period and the rest period must be completed in a specific time. This type of training typically incorporates higher repetitions with shorter rest periods.

duration—Time allotted for each rep, set, or workout.

eccentric phase—Action of the muscle lengthening during its contraction; eccentric phase as it applies to plyometrics is the *loading* phase of the drill.

fast-twitch fibers—The type of white (light) muscle tissue that is used during explosive movements for strength, power, and speed.

frequency—How many times (per day, week, and so forth) you work out.

golgi tendon organ—Receptors located where the muscle fuses with the tendon (for example, musculotendinous junction). The golgi tendon organ provides very precise information concerning the tension of the muscle and serves as a protective mechanism to prevent the tendon from rupture as a result of a forceful contraction. To prevent injury, the golgi tendon initiates an immediate relaxation of the muscle when too much tension occurs.

hypertrophy—Enlargement of muscle-fiber types as a result of specific training adaptations.

in-season—Term applied to strength training performed throughout the competitive schedule when games are being played.

intensity—Effort level exerted while performing an exercise. The intensity of a workout can be changed by changing the exercise order, or increasing or decreasing the number of exercises, repetitions, weight, or rest periods.

major muscle groups—The following groups of muscles are considered the major muscle groups of the body: chest, shoulders, back, hips, and thighs.

muscle balance—Training opposing muscle groups with the same intensity to prevent injury and enhance performance.

muscle movements and contractions

> **eccentric contraction**—Lengthening of a muscle during an exercise, for example, the lowering of the bar during a biceps curl, which lengthens the biceps muscle.
>
> **isokinetic**—The speed of movement remains constant no matter how intense the contraction. This type of movement is the result of work on resistance machines that use pistons, shocks, and cylinders.
>
> **isometric**—When both ends of a muscle are fixed and no joint movement occurs; physiological work is being done, but not physical work.
>
> **isotonic/concentric contraction**—Shortening of a muscle during an exercise, for example, the raising of the bar during a biceps curl that shortens the biceps muscle.

muscle spindle/stretch receptors—Located in, among, and parallel to the muscle fibers are small spindle-shaped mechanisms that sense the rate and length of a stretched muscle.

muscular endurance—Ability to perform movements over an extended period.

off-season—Term applied to strength training performed in the noncompetitive season. Twelve weeks before preseason is the standard used in this book.

overload—A phase of training that goes beyond the initial output level: overloading the training level by increasing the intensity or duration of an exercise. See intensity.

overtraining—Breakdown in the recovery process that may be attributed to mental attitude, lack of sleep or rest, improper eating habits, and overuse of the body.

postseason—Time immediately after the season (two to eight weeks); usually called active rest.

power—Can be measured by calculating a formula: force times distance divided by time.

power lifting—Weightlifting in which the sum (one-rep maximum) of three separate weight-training lifts—squat, bench, and dead lift—are totaled.

prepubescent weight training—Training associated with young athletes before puberty. To reduce the potential risk of injury, repetitions for each exercise should range from 12 to 15 and sets should be limited to two or three.

preseason—Period from the first practice until the first game.

progression—Phase of training in which the intensity of a workout is increased.

range of motion—Refers to the specific range of motion suggested while performing an exercise.

repetition—A fully completed movement of the exercise.

set—Each time an exercise is performed for a given number of repetitions.

target sets—Quality, hard-working, high-intensity sets that follow warm-up sets; each exercise should consist of at least one to two target sets.

warm-up sets—Sets performed to prevent injury and increase the temperature of the muscles and surrounding tissues.

stabilizer—Usually a nonmoving isometric contraction stabilizing one body part so that another body part, usually involving the prime mover, has something to pull against to create the movement; for example, in leg lifts, the abdominal muscles are stabilized while the hip flexors are the prime movers.

stretch reflex—The stretch or myotatic reflex results in the reflex contraction of a muscle after it has been rapidly stretched. When a muscle is rapidly stretched, as occurs during the eccentric or loading phase of a plyometric drill, the muscle spindles discharge impulses, resulting in a reflex contraction of the stretched muscle. An example of the stretch reflex is the knee-jerk test. When the patellar ligament is tapped, the muscle spindles located in the quadriceps femoris send a message to the spine which in turn sends a message back to the quads instructing them to contract.

super setting—Performing two or more exercises one after the other before a rest period is taken; a super set can be performed with exercises for opposing muscle groups, for the same muscle group, or for nonassociated muscle groups.

synergist/assistance muscle—Aids the prime mover with the movement.

total-body joint exercise—Movements, explosive in nature, that involve the ankle, knee, hip, and shoulder joints.

volume—Total number of repetitions performed in a given workout.

warm-up, general—Usually uses large muscle groups and nonspecific movements to bring out desired physiological changes.

warm-up, specific—Duplicates the exact movement or exercise to be performed with very light weight and high repetitions.

weightlifting—The type of weight training incorporating the Olympic lifts—the clean and jerk and the snatch.

REFERENCES

Alter, Michael J. *Sport Stretch.* Champaign, IL: Human Kinetics, 1990.

American Dairy Council. *Power Food Handout.* 1993.

Baechle, T. and the NSCA. *Essentials of Strength Training and Conditioning.* Champaign, IL: Human Kinetics, 1994.

Briggs, G., and D. Calloway. *Nutrition and Physical Fitness.* 11th ed. Ft. Worth, TX: Holt, Rinehart & Winston, 1984.

Clark, Nancy. *Nancy Clark's Sports Nutrition Guidebook.* Champaign, IL: Leisure Press, 1990.

Clark, Nancy. *Nancy Clark's Sports Nutrition Guidebook.* 2nd ed. Champaign, IL: Human Kinetics, 1997.

Fox, E.L., and D.K. Matthews. *Physiological Basis of Physical Education and Athletics.* 3rd ed. Philadelphia: Saunders, 1981.

Guyton, A. *Textbook of Medical Physiology.* 7th ed. Philadelphia, PA: W.B. Saunders, 1986.

Hickson, J.F. *Nutrition in Exercise and Sport.* Boca Raton, FL: CRC Press, 1989.

Knortz, Karen, and C. Ringel. "Flexibility Techniques," *NSCA Journal* 7, no. 2 (1985).

McAtee, Robert E. *Facilitated Stretching.* Champaign, IL: Human Kinetics, 1993.

Siff, Mel C. "As a System of Physical Conditioning." *National Strength and Conditioning Association Journal* 13, no. 4 (1991).

Stone, Michael, and H. O'Bryant. *Weight Training: A Scientific Approach.* Edina, MN: Burgess International, 1987.

ABOUT THE NBCCA

The National Basketball Conditioning Coaches Association (NBCCA) is a select group of strength and conditioning coaches from teams in the National Basketball Association. The NBCCA was founded in 1992 by Bill Foran of the Miami Heat, Robin Pound of the Phoenix Suns, and Bob King then of the Dallas Mavericks. The association's mission is to develop and promote strength and conditioning throughout basketball, particularly at the professional level. The NBCCA provides an opportunity for strength and conditioning coaches in the league to network, keep updated on new information, work together on different projects, and promote strength and conditioning for basketball at all levels.

Bill Foran—Strength and conditioning coach for the Miami Heat. Bill, who acted as project coordinator for *NBA Power Conditioning* along with Robin Pound of the Phoenix Suns, currently lives in Pembroke Pines, Florida with his wife and two children. He earned a bachelor's degree in health education and physical education from Central Michigan University and a master's degree in exercise physiology from Michigan State University. Before working for the Miami Heat, Bill was the head strength and conditioning coach at Washington State University and University of Miami. He is a Certified Strength and Conditioning Specialist and enjoys working out and traveling. Bill was co-founder of the National Basketball Conditioning Coaches Association and coordinated all sections of *NBA Power Conditioning*.

Robin Pound—Strength and conditioning coach for the Phoenix Suns. Robin, who along with Bill Foran of the Miami Heat acted as project coordinator for *NBA Power Conditioning*, lives in Phoenix, Arizona. He earned a bachelor's degree in physical education and a teaching degree from the University of Oregon where he also earned a master's degree in exercise physiology and anatomy. Before working for the Phoenix Suns, Robin worked as the assistant strength and conditioning coach for the University of Oregon and then as head strength and conditioning coach at the University of California at Berkeley. Robin, who enjoys staying fit and healthy and being in the outdoors, is co-founder of the National Basketball Conditioning Coaches Association and currently sits on the Board of Directors of that association. Robin coordinated all sections of *NBA Power Conditioning* and specifically worked on the Strength Training and Strength-Training Programs chapters.

Al Biancani—Strength and conditioning coach for the Sacramento Kings. Al lives in Citrus Heights, California with his wife. He earned a bachelor's and master's degree from California State University at Sacramento in physical education. He then earned a doctorate in physical education curriculum and supervision from Utah State University. Besides working for the Sacramento Kings, Al owns his own fitness training business where he is a personal trainer and an off-season strength and conditioning coach for professional, college, and high school football, baseball, basketball, soccer, and boxing. He is a Certified Strength and Conditioning Specialist and was chapter coordinator and writer for the Speed Training chapter.

Sol Brandys—Strength and conditioning coach for the Minnesota Timberwolves. Sol lives with his wife and son in Deephaven, Minnesota. Before working for the Minnesota Timberwolves, Sol was a strength and conditioning consultant for the University of Minnesota athletic department and an executive for Northwest Health Clubs. He has also worked with many professional athletes from a wide variety of sports including baseball and tennis. Sol, who has been a life-long resident of Minneapolis, earned a bachelor's degree from the University of Minnesota in physical education. He was the chapter coordinator and writer for the Power Conditioning Base chapter.

Mark Grabow—Strength and conditioning coach for the Golden State Warriors. Mark lives in Lafayette, California with his wife. He earned a bachelor's degree in psychology from American University, Washington, D.C. Along with working for Golden State, Mark works as a conditioning coach for Pete Newell's Big Man camp and as a consultant for the Japanese National team, Lithuanian Olympic team, and the Stanford Men's and women's team. He was a writer for the agility chapter.

Dennis L. Householder—Strength and conditioning coach for the Washington Wizards. Dennis lives in Crofton, Maryland with his wife. He earned a bachelor's degree in physical education from Shepherd College in West Virginia. Before working for the Washington Wizards, Dennis worked as a high school football coach in Maryland and in numerous health clubs and spas. He was a writer for the Strength Training chapter.

Bob Medina—Strength and conditioning coach for the Seattle SuperSonics. Bob lives with his wife in Seattle, Washington. With a bachelor's degree in athletic training and a minor in health education from University of Nevada at Las Vegas, Bob worked for UNLV as an assistant strength and conditioning coach for all sports as an undergraduate. After graduating, he worked as a full-time assistant strength and conditioning coach for UNLV for three seasons. He was a writer for the Power Conditioning Base chapter.

David Oliver—Strength and conditioning coach for the Orlando Magic. David lives with his wife and son in Orlando, Florida. Previous to working for the Orlando Magic, David worked at the University of Wisconsin as an athletic trainer and at the Orlando Sports Medicine Center. He earned a bachelor's degree from the University of Wisconsin in exercise physiology. He is a Certified Strength and Conditioning Specialist as well as a Certified Athletic Trainer. David was the chapter coordinator and writer for the Stretching, Warm-Up, and Cool-Down chapter.

Chip Sigmon—Strength and conditioning coach for the Charlotte Hornets. Chip lives with his wife and daughter in Charlotte, North Carolina. He earned a bachelor's degree in physical education from Appalachian State University in Boone, North Carolina. Before working for the Charlotte Hornets, Chip worked as the strength and conditioning coach at Appalachian State University. Chip was a writer for the Power Conditioning Base chapter.

Mick Smith—Strength and conditioning coach for the Portland Trail Blazers. Mick lives in Lake Oswego, Oregon with his wife and son. Before working for the Portland Trail Blazers, Mick worked as the strength and conditioning coach for Creighton University and Christopher Columbus High School, Miami, Florida, and as assistant strength and conditioning coach for the University of Miami. He earned a bachelor's degree in physical education and health education and a master's degree in exercise science from the University of Nebraska at Omaha. He is a Certified Strength and Conditioning Specialist and was a writer for the Strength Training chapter.

More basketball books

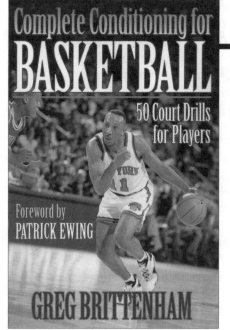

1996 • Paperback • 264 pp
Item PBRI0881
ISBN 0-87322-881-2
$15.95 ($23.95 Canadian)

Shows how to design a specific program that will improve speed, power, endurance, agility, coordination, balance, and reaction time. Includes 15 flexibility exercises, 9 exercises for abdominal and lower back, 9 movement patterns, 11 fitness tests, and 12 sample workouts. Provides guidelines and charts for developing a personalized training program.

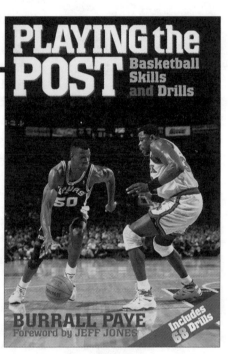

1996 • Paperback • 256 pp
Item PPAY0979
ISBN0-87322-979-7
$15.95 ($22.95 Canadian)

Details everything players and coaches need to know to create a strong inside game. Includes 68 drills and exercises, and features 10 principles for scoring from the post, 12 drills for scoring from the high and low post, 8 drills to improve rebounding, 7 drills to improve post passing, 24 techniques for defending the post position, and 10 advanced moves.

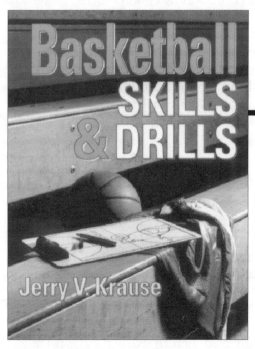

1991 • Paperback • 136 pp
Item PKRA0422
ISBN 0-88011-422-3
$16.95 ($23.95 Canadian)

Explains fundamentals to start beginners off right and reinforce basic skills in more advanced players. Part I covers individual basketball skills, including basic position, ballhandling, moves without the ball, shooting, perimeter moves, post moves, defense, and rebounding. Part II deals with game preparation and strategy, plus offensive and defensive tactics.

Prices subject to change.

Human Kinetics
The Premier Publisher for Sports & Fitness
www.humankinetics.com

2335

To request more information or to place your order,
U.S. customers call **TOLL-FREE 1-800-747-4457**.
Customers outside the U.S. use appropriate telephone
number/address shown in the front of this book.

8/99